LOUDER VOICES:

The Corporate Welfare Bums

DAVID LEWIS

With an introduction by Eric Kierans

James Lewis & Samuel, Toronto, 1972

ISBN 0-88862-031-4

Printed in Canada
by Ronalds-Federated

James Lewis & Samuel, Publishers
35 Britain Street
Toronto 229, Canada

Printed and bound in Canada

Contents

		PAGE
Preface		v
Introduction / Eric Kierans		vi
1.	The Corporate Welfare State	1
2.	One City, Two Worlds	12
3.	The Extractive Industries	17
4.	The Land Envelopers	38
5.	Solutions of the Past	62
6.	Alphabet Soup	72
7.	Participatory Tax Reform	97
8.	Beyond the Corporate Welfare State	104

Reprinted with permission of the *Toronto Star*

"Buddy, can you spare a million?"

And I concede your point too, that it's likely we heard more from the vested interests than we did from the little taxpayer who didn't have . . . the high-paid lawyers to speak for him . . . I suppose in participatory democracy there will always be some whose voice is louder than others . . ."

— Pierre Trudeau, speaking on the white paper on taxation, CTV, December 28, 1971

PREFACE

For many years, democratic socialists have recognized that despite Canada's enormous wealth and the native compassion of its people, gross inequities have continued to exist in our social and economic structure. We have laboured to make Canadians aware of these inequities. We have voiced them in Parliament; we have fought for legislation to correct them; we have knocked on doors to tell the people, and we have worked with other concerned organizations in the struggle to make our message understood, so that Canadians would take action to bring an end to these inequities.

Our message is not new. It is one of commitment to social and economic justice that others have shared for centuries. Perhaps the new element about our message is that we have found a way to help people understand. We have given them the information, the precise and irrefutable evidence they need to comprehend fully the extent of injustice in this great country.

It has been a difficult undertaking, but the rewards have been many. We know now that people are listening, becoming aware, judging. And this is the first step in the struggle to eliminate those injustices that no humane society will knowingly tolerate.

Months of research have gone into compiling the evidence on which we base our case against free-enterprise governments and their corporate allies. I cannot adequately express my gratitude to the many dedicated people who have contributed so much time and effort.

I would like to extend special thanks to NDP Research Director Boris Celovsky; to Peter Sadler-Brown, David Kelly, Veronica Seale, Nancy Tienhaara, Richard Kerr, Fran McKenna and Wendy Cuthbertson, and the many others who helped document the facts that led to the writing of this book.

DAVID LEWIS
Toronto

September 24, 1972

Introduction

I was very pleased indeed to receive an invitation from David Lewis to write an introduction to this book, which expands upon many of the themes and issues that he has raised during this election campaign. Every Canadian, whether he agrees with the New Democratic Party leader or not, is in his debt for having discussed fundamental economic problems facing this nation and thus ensuring that the present election will be fought on issues that demand solutions, and not on simple generalizations.

Rather than deal lightly with all subjects treated in this publication, I would like to concentrate on the substance of the charges that are incorporated in Mr. Lewis's colourful way of communicating with the Canadian people, that is, in his description of "corporate ripoffs," "corporate welfare bums," etc.

Already, the campaign has drawn flat denials from the government. Both the prime minister and the minister of Finance have stated that Mr. Lewis's charges are no longer relevant; they have said specifically that the deferred tax liabilities will eventually come due and that, in any event, the tax-reform bill of 1971 has eliminated these abuses. Both statements are simply untrue.

In the first place, the tax-reform bill did not touch in any way the granting of capital-cost allowances, greatly in excess of real depreciation, as a charge against profits. Secondly, in a growing economy the absolute amount of tax deferrals must grow over time. It is only if we contemplate a depression of the severity and duration of the thirties that we can visualize a decline in capital expenditures of such magnitude that the real depreciation of Canada's productive plant would exceed the capital-cost allowances permitted by the Income Tax Act. In that event, the corporate economy would be unable to find the cash to pay its back taxes anyway, without thousands of firms going bankrupt.

A little history. In 1969, Walter E. Duffett, the Dominion statistician, announced a new series of reports to replace *Taxation Statistics Part 2—Corporations,* previously published by the Taxation Division of the Department of National Revenue. From 1965 on, taxation statistics were to be published in two volumes, *Corporation Taxation Statistics* and *Corporation Financial Statistics*.

Mr. Duffett's own explanation for the changes is worth drawing to the attention of readers.

> During the early part of the twenty-year period that the Department of National Revenue compiled financial statistics on corporations, *corporation profit was essentially the same as taxable income and therefore it was possible to satisfy both needs with one set of statistics.* However, during this period (1944–1964) and particularly during the last decade, taxation legislation, through special provisions, has been used to an increasing extent as an instrument of government policy. As this use of taxation legislation was extended, the relationship between corporation profit and taxable income became dependent upon the degree to which corporations utilized these provisions. During this period corporation taxable income has been affected by the industry in which the firm operates, the scope of the firm's operations, the geographical location, the ownership of the firm and several other factors. As a result, it was becoming increasingly difficult to use the same information to satisfy the needs for data of both corporation finance generally and corporation income taxation.*

In effect, corporation financial statistics were presented by the corporation in one form to its shareholders and in quite a different form to the Department of Revenue for tax purposes. One of the major areas of difference was the accounting for depreciation of assets. The shareholders were given a more or less real figure for such decline in values. The government was given an inflated figure, with its full knowledge, that helped to reduce profits substantially and hence the immediate tax liability.

It is this that Mr. Lewis is talking about and, the prime minister's and the minister of Finance's statements to the contrary, this was not changed, altered or modified in the slightest by the so-called tax-reform legislation. They are not being untruthful or insincere but simply accepting wrong information from officials in the Department of Finance and/or their own advisors.

The proof is in the white paper itself. After explaining why

Corporation Taxation Statistics (Ottawa, 1965), introduction.

there would be *no change* in the system of capital-cost allowances despite the "cost in government revenue," paragraph 14 of chapter 5 of the white paper goes on to say:

> Nevertheless some have suggested that they are too generous, and the government believes that after 20 years of the system it is time for a review. However, depreciation is an important aspect of the tax system and taxpayers should have an opportunity to put forward their views and experience before major changes are considered. Therefore, the government intends in due course to invite briefs on the system and rates of capital-cost allowance.

There has been no review. There have been no changes except to worsen the situation as I will discuss later. While Mr. Lewis's figures deal with the sixties, as the prime minister and minister of Finance have pointed out, they are the only figures available. But the exact same state of affairs obtains today. When Mr. Lewis speaks of $3.2 billion in corporate income taxes unpaid, at no interest cost, in 1969, I would estimate that this amount will be approximately $4.7 billion at the end of this year. Of this amount, about $3.2 billion will have benefitted the two hundred-odd corporations with assets of more than $100 million and about $25 million will have been received by the 160,000 corporations with assets of less than $250,000. The new firm, of course, gets nothing. Its loans carry the normal bank or IDB rates.

The review promised in the white paper never did get off the ground. Within days of its publication, Mr. Benson backed away from chapter 5, paragraph 14. "Mr. Benson, however, stated on November 20, 1969, in Vancouver in public and before the press that he did not think that any downward changes in capital-cost allowances were merited. He said that the review suggested in paragraph 5.14 was prompted by the thought that in some areas CCA rates might be too low."*

For the record, may I say, as a continuing and active member of the Tax Reform Cabinet Committee during this period, that paragraph 14 was not inserted because members believed that capital-cost allowances were too low. The paragraph itself refutes this.

---

*D. H. Parkinson, C.A., *Report on White Paper Conference* (Canadian Tax Foundation, 1970), p. 273.

This quick and easy capitulation by the minister of Finance on CCA rates gave heart to all the opponents of the white paper. They stormed to the attack, particularly in the area of reform of taxation on business and property income. As a result, the final bill was a pale imitation of the white paper, which itself had only a pallid resemblance to the Carter commission report.

This situation has worsened, not improved. Keeping capital-cost allowance rates at the same level, Mr. Benson in 1970 altered the amount of capital expenditures that could be written off against profits. Gone was the concept that a cost is a cost. For every $3 million that a mining company invested in new plant and equipment, they could put down as the cost, for tax purposes, not $3 million but $4 million, an addition to costs without any basis in reality. In December 1970, he gave manufacturing companies the right to price their investment expenditures at 115 per cent of their cost. Mr. Duffett must have been tearing his hair out by the roots. A cost is not a cost when it is padded. And what does a poor statistician do?

If individual taxpayers were to pad their charitable donations by an extra 15 per cent or 33⅓ per cent, they would find them disallowed and heavy fines imposed for false reporting. Not so with corporations. It is all quite legal.

Perhaps, on the principle that what his predecessor could do, he could do better, Mr. Turner upped the ante. On May 8 of this year, he said that all machinery and equipment acquired after budget day for manufacturing and processing could be written off in two years, i.e., a machine with a twenty-year life, depreciable at the rate of 5 per cent a year, could be written off at a rate of 50 per cent per year and charged off entirely to profits in two years.

How many times can incentives such as these be introduced before the well of new investments runs dry? And at what cost to the revenues of the country? How do you measure the distortions in an economy when you subsidize the use of capital, of which Canada is short, and discriminate against the employment of labour, of which we have a surplus?

The situation has not improved as the government says since the tax reform bill; it has, I repeat, grown worse.

The Department of Finance does not want any review of capital-cost allowances or Mr. Lewis's charges. It is desperate for it knows that it has a tiger by the tail; the amount is growing year by year. At the end of the seventies, *the amount of interest-free loans*, given the expanding capital expenditures during this decade, could reach $12 billion, mainly to a few hundred large corporations. Even the corporations themselves are beginning to worry. Liabilities of such magnitude are crippling, even when they are deferred. These huge amounts hang like the sword of Damocles over their future planning.

The government could take an equity position for the amount of taxes due in the larger corporations. Or it could charge a bank-rate of interest on the amounts outstanding. Or take interest-bearing bonds with a definite redemption date. Or it could forgive the taxes owing. But would the ordinary taxpayer stand for that? There is a real dilemma here, and the longer the government runs away from the problem, the worse it becomes.

Before anything else, it must make up its mind to abandon the distinction between capital-cost allowances and the costs of real depreciation. A cost is a cost, not something more or something less. Walter Duffett, when he was forced to issue two sets of corporation statistics, and David Lewis today are saying the same thing.

In concluding, I want to say something on behalf of my own party, the Liberal Party. The tax policies criticized in this introduction are not policies that have emanated from the party itself. Most members would abhor these special privileges, exemptions and concessions as much as I do. They originate in that most stagnant of all Ottawa bureaucracies, the Department of Finance. It is time that the party itself came to the rescue of the government, with new ideas and policies designed to resolve the many problems our country faces.

But until that time comes, many of us will follow Mr. Lewis's efforts to inject some realism into this electoral campaign with a great deal of respect and considerable admiration.

ERIC KIERANS
Montreal

September 27, 1972

CHAPTER ONE

The Corporate Welfare State

The corporate welfare state is not a new phenomenon, despite the notoriety it has achieved only recently. Unlike its counterpart, the social welfare state, its gestation period has been largely unobserved by interpreters of social events. And while social welfare legislation has been subjected to the most critical scrutiny as to its costs, benefits and consequences, the attention of Canadians has been deflected from any examination of the other face of the mixed economy, Canadian-style: the corporate welfare state.

The nature of the corporate welfare state has been obscured by the traditional moralizing of big business about the virtues of free enterprise. While they publicly denounce increased government expenditure, particularly in the form of social welfare, these champions of free enterprise actively lobby the government for incentive grants, research grants and tax concessions, and all manner of assistance at the individual taxpayer's expense. And because they have drawn a sympathetic response from Liberal and Conservative governments, which subscribe to the myth of "business confidence," their appetite for welfare continues to increase.

The traditional use of the term "mixed economy" acknowledges the co-existence of private and public enterprise within one society. In Canada, the mixed economy has advanced beyond the co-existence of the public and private spheres: it has reached the stage where private business is increasingly being supported by the public purse. As a result, Canadian businesses, whatever their public pronouncements on the matter, not only acquiesce to government involvement in the economy but have come to depend upon it. Their "welfare cheques," in the form of grants and tax concessions, have become an integral aspect of their operation.

The corporate welfare state did not emerge overnight. We may be inclined to regard the establishment of the Department of Regional Economic Expansion (DREE) in 1969 as the birthdate of business government, simply because the handouts to business during the past four years have dwarfed all previous programs. However it would be far more appropriate to view the establishment of DREE as the blossoming of our mixed-economy hybrid, whose roots go back through several administrations, from Trudeau to Pearson to Diefenbaker to St. Laurent.

During the depression that followed the First World War, economists, notably John Maynard Keynes, developed a theory that depressions need not occur if governments were able to bring about a high level of investment and consumption, either through the private sector or through government expenditures. After the Second World War the Liberal government feared another recession would occur when spending on the war ceased. To avoid this, they chose to stimulate private investment rather than rely on purchases of goods and services by individual consumers. Since that time every subsequent government has copied its predecessor and returned again and again to the same economic approach. Having reluctantly given up the old economic orthodoxy of the pre-war years, these governments have created a new orthodoxy to which they subscribe with as little reflection or imagination as did the dinosaurs of the thirties. As soon as the economy slows down, Ottawa provides incentives for capital investment.

In his June 3, 1971, address to the Canadian Economic Association, Eric Kierans, former minister of Communications in the Trudeau government, was highly critical of Ottawa's obsession with private investment in capital goods as the prime economic stimulus:

> The difficulty is that Ottawa still sees the role of private investment as being as important a determinant of growth in income and employment as Keynes made it when he wrote *The General Theory* in the depths of the depression . . .
>
> We do have, however, as a result of Keynes, the world of the 60s and 70s that he despaired of ever seeing in democracies except in time of war. When governments in Canada themselves demand approximately 22 per cent of the output of goods and services in the economy and tax away about 35 per cent of national product to pay for goods and services as well as to redistribute income from the affluent to the poor, then *we have a strong built-in inducement for private investment to respond to this expanding demand.*

2

Declining investment opportunities and a weakening marginal propensity to consume are no longer the nightmares that Keynes feared. With governments faced with huge social needs in housing, control of the environment and pollution, health and welfare services, etc., an expanding volume of effective demand exists to which investment *can and will respond naturally*. [italics added]

Despite this demand for goods, which is evident to everybody, especially the individual consumer, the governments of the recent past have continued to provide incentives to business so that private investment will be channelled into economic hardware, new plants, new machinery, new technology. Rather than allowing investment to flow naturally to areas of real demand and real need, these governments have distorted the Canadian economy by dogmatically pursuing a rigid orthodoxy that would affront and appal Keynes himself. Moreover, their dogmatism tends to escalate rather than abate, the further their activities stray from reality. The very substance of programs like the Department of Regional Economic Expansion has been not to deal with real regional disparity and inequality, but to become a temple of economic religion at which the faithful may worship.

The religion of capital investment has been the motivating force behind the creation of the corporate welfare state. To induce capital investment, the post-war governments have looked for and have found virtually every means imaginable to provide incentives. The most important, because it is the most costly to the individual taxpayer, is the use of tax incentives and grants.

The most generous tax incentive is the capital-cost allowance —a deduction from corporate earnings permitted in the calculation of tax payments. The allowable deduction is a percentage of the original cost of a piece of equipment or a building, which in theory reflects its rate of deterioration. The real rate of deterioration is usually not nearly as high as that represented in the capital-cost allowance. This is clear from the fact that when corporations report to their shareholders, a much slower rate of depreciation is used to calculate net income. Because corporations are allowed to deduct unrealis-

3

tically high capital-cost allowances, their taxes paid in the years immediately after on investment are lower than they should be. The taxes paid towards the end of the life of a piece of equipment are correspondingly higher than would be paid using realistic depreciation rates. The net result is a postponing of tax payments—in effect, a loan to the corporation without any requirement for repayment with interest.

Since 1949, Canadian governments have been tinkering with rates of capital-cost allowances in order to stimulate the purchase of new equipment; in other words, to encourage capital investment. If a business can get a higher deduction from its income tax by being permitted a faster write-off on its equipment, it has an incentive to buy new equipment. A new system of allowances was introduced in Canada in 1949 that departed from straight-line depreciation, which had allowed deductions for each year's portion of wear and tear. The diminishing-balance principle created the fiction that most wear and tear occurs early in the life of the equipment; businesses were therefore allowed to deduct as an expense the greatest portion of the cost of a piece of equipment in the early years of its use. This procedure, of course, releases a significant amount of money to the business as a tax saving; it was for this explicit reason that the system had been introduced in Britain. However, it is difficult to justify the Canadian version in terms of the British precedent; the practice was introduced there to assist industries bombed out in the war.

In December 1960, the government, now Conservative, tinkered again with the capital-cost allowances rates. Double depreciation was allowed on fixed assets acquired during 1961 over the years 1961, 1962 and 1963. The rationale for this tax advantage was: (1) to assist new industries "in areas where there is a substantial degree of continued unemployment over the years"; (2) to aid the development of "new products from processing operations not hitherto carried on in Canada"; and (3) to "encourage the production of new types of goods."*

With the new wave of Liberal-style nationalism, personified by Lester Pearson's first minister of Finance, Walter Gordon, an attempt was made to manipulate capital-cost allowances in favour of Canadian business. "Firms who were 25 per cent

*J. Harvey Perry, *Taxation in Canada*, 3rd ed. (Toronto: University of Toronto Press, 1961), p. 70.

Canadian owned were allowed to write off new equipment in two years, 50 per cent per year. Those firms which located in designated areas were allowed to write off new buildings in five years.*

The Trudeau government, in dogged pursuit of the course set by its predecessors, has similarly used capital-cost allowances for economic stimulus. Edgar Benson's amended Income Tax Act, Section 13(10), provides that machinery, equipment and certain buildings acquired by a manufacturing or processing enterprise may be deemed under some circumstances to have been purchased at 115 per cent of their actual cost for the purpose of calculating capital-cost allowances. John Turner's budget of 1972 permits a two-year write-off of the cost of machinery for manufacturing and processing, in other words, a 50 per cent rate of capital-cost allowances per year.

Capital-cost allowances are not the only concessions given to corporations, but they are the most significant in economic terms. Besides draining revenue from the government, they introduce a bias in the direction of our economic growth. As a result, the individual Canadian is hit two ways. In the first place, individual taxpayers have had to make up for revenue losses incurred by the higher allowances to corporations. In 1951, corporate direct taxes amounted to 28 per cent of all revenues collected by the federal government. Individuals contributed 26.7 per cent. By 1973, according to John Turner's budget, individual taxpayers will provide 49.9 per cent of government revenues, while corporations will make up only 12.2 per cent.

Secondly, the individual has been forced to suffer the consequences of the economic bias created by government tinkering with the capital-cost allowance system. By encouraging private investment in capital equipment and by ignoring the need to reduce the economic pressures on the individual by cutting his taxes (if only to compensate for higher interest rates induced by the investment booms), governments of the past fifteen years have actively contributed to inflation and instability in the economy. Eric Kierans has defined the eco-

*Eric Kierans, Address to the Canadian Economic Association, Memorial University, St. John's, Newfoundland (June 3, 1971), mimeographed, p. 6.

nomic dilemma of the Diefenbaker years:

> Canadians never did get the advantage of the productivity inherent in their increased capital stock by the longer runs and lower costs that expanded demand, domestic and export, would have given them. The capacity was there, both physical and human, but the demand was shut off by a monetary policy that worked in the opposite direction to the fiscal incentives. Operating at less than capacity, the inflexibility of excess investment in plant and equipment and overhead costs had to be worked off and prices remained sticky and even rose during the period.*

The Canadian economy followed the same pattern in the mid-sixties under the Pearson government. After Walter Gordon's budget of 1963, another investment boom in capital expenditures took place. Again, as in the early sixties, interest rates rose and investment in housing declined. "The large decline in housing starts in the face of overwhelming needs added to the scarcity and became one of the key elements in rising prices and unemployment. Canada exchanged investment in housing for investment in machinery."**

That the Trudeau government is bent upon taking the same course as its predecessors is beyond understanding. Lack of experience with this economic phenomenon can, to some extent, exonerate earlier governments. Commitment to Keynesian economic theory had been undertaken with some reluctance, with the result that Keynes was interpreted in such a way that his theory would be most directly and immediately favourable to private businesses. This interpretation—that counter-cyclical trends to economic decline can be best induced by private investment in capital expenditure—has become religion to recent governments. No amount of empirical data have been able to dissuade the present government from this entrenched belief.

To the range of tax incentives has now been added a vast network of direct welfare to corporations. Thus, the individual taxpayer must now not only make up for revenue losses incurred by tax concessions, but also pay directly for corporate capital expenditures.

---

*Kierans, p. 5.
**Kierans, p. 7.

The Department of Regional Economic Expansion represents the culmination of those forces of the past twenty years which have veered Canada in the direction of the corporate welfare state. Because the governments of the sixties allowed themselves to become locked into a particular economic point of view, it was almost inevitable that they would reach the point of distributing welfare handouts to corporations. This state of affairs reflects a sincerity on their part that they were creating jobs, and so they remain, despite all arguments and evidence to the contrary, steadfast in their sincerity and in their error. By ignoring the areas of demand in the economy, particularly in housing, their economic remedies have become equivalent to throwing buckets of water on a drowning man. Their mistake lies in believing this to be the only solution, if it is a solution at all.

The origins of DREE are rooted in the recognition of economic disparity and inequality in Canada. The precursor to the Regional Development Incentives Act, the Area Development Incentives Act (ADIA) was made operative in 1965 in order to develop areas of Canada that suffered lower levels of income and opportunity than the rest of the country. Admitting that tax incentives like capital-cost allowances to businesses had not solved the problem of economic inequality, the minister of Industry of the day, the Hon. C. M. Drury, announced that the government would offer "cash grants to new manufacturing and processing firms establishing in designated areas, as well as to firms expanding their existing facilities. The amounts of these grants are to be directly related to the total investment in fixed assets made by these enterprises." The amount of the grant was based on a rate of one-third of the first $250,000 of eligible capital costs, plus one-quarter of the next $750,000, plus one-fifth of any remaining capital cost, with a maximum limit of $5 million per project. Furthermore, approved projects were also eligible for accelerated capital-cost allowance, thereby reducing the amount of income tax payable.

There were a number of problems with the ADIA program, the most important of which was that expansion in capital facilities is no guarantee that jobs will be created. The Regional Development Incentives Act of 1969, to be administered by the new Department of Regional Economic Expansion, was designed to solve that problem by tying grants to the number of jobs created. In its annual report of 1969–1970, DREE optimistically announced that "the new Regional Development Incentives legislation, which became effective July 1, 1969, *quickly gave promise of greater effectiveness* than the ADIA program in attracting new industries to slow-growth regions." The implication that ADIA was not showing all the promise that the government's economic orthodoxy had decreed did not lead the government to re-examine its theories, but only to introduce some modifications into its style of handouts.

ADIA was run on the naïve basis of a flat-rate subsidy to investment in capital expenditure because it was believed that this would naturally and by itself create jobs. The Hon. Jean Marchand, minister of Regional Economic Expansion, explained the greater sophistication of the new program to the House of Commons in June 1969:

> A clearer way of expressing the purpose of the program, however, is to measure the whole incentive in terms of the jobs created. In an industry using an average amount of capital, we will be prepared to provide an incentive up to $12,000 for each new job created. If the industry is one that uses a lot of capital, we will go as high as $30,000 per job. I should make it plain that while the incentive will now be related to the employment created as well as to the amount of the investment, the proposed program is, just as much as ADA [Area Development Agency] has been, a program of capital incentives.

From then on the cost of the job was to be assessed on money provided for its creation according to the type of industry being developed. Mr. Marchand recognized the absurdity of flat-rate grants when he said:

> If we paid the maximum level of them all, we would in some cases be wasting the taxpayers' money. We would be providing some companies with more incentive than they really need, *and the difference would be a windfall profit at public expense*.

One can only speculate on the size of the windfalls gained by corporations during the four years of ADIA's operation.

However, Mr. Marchand's new program of tying grants to the number of jobs created suffers from one fundamental fallacy. Businesses depend upon markets to survive. If they cannot sell the goods they produce, no amount of capital expenditure is going to rescue the operation or the jobs. Inattention to common-sense planning has led to such fiascos as occurred in the pulp and paper industry. In January 1971, DREE provided $15 million in incentive grants to Procter and Gamble Canada Ltd., to build a mill in Grande Prairie, Alberta, to produce bleached kraft paper. In January 1972, the department gave $13.8 million to Rayonnier Quebec Inc. (ITT), to build a pulp mill near Port Cartier, Quebec. Because the pulp markets had been poor, even while the government was providing money to build new mills, an existing firm in Temiscamingue, Quebec, was driven out of business with the result that 875 persons lost their jobs. Indeed, there were layoffs in most other pulp operations.

An experience with the Michelin Tire Corporation is a striking example of the degree of insecurity of jobs created by the government's welfare handouts. Michelin was provided with $15 million by the federal government under DREE and ADIA, and was also granted tax remissions when it located its operation in Pictou, Nova Scotia. The Nova Scotia government provided a $50-million loan at an interest rate of only 6 per cent and gave it a $9-million grant to boot. Upon its threatened exclusion from US markets, Michelin stated in a submission to the US Commissioner of Customs that *all these grants had little to do with its decision to build in Pictou County*. It also said, in the same submission, that it would build new factories in the United States which would result in "a substantial reduction in the shipments [of Michelin tires] from Canada to the US," and that "ultimately it is likely that Michelin's Canadian plants will serve mainly Canada."

If Michelin fails to find markets in Canada that can sustain the employment of one thousand workers, all the investments made by the taxpayers of Canada will be worthless. The public has no equity and no guarantee about the future of any of the jobs that are created by the $600 million that their government gives away to corporations every year. This figure is based only on the direct grants. The give-aways resulting from tax holidays, concessions and remissions are almost incalculable. For example, of the approximately 200,000 corporations in Canada, half do not pay any income tax at all.

9

DREE has not been the success that the government would have the public believe. In 1969, the Hon. Jean Marchand spoke hopefully of eliminating the term *slow growth* from many regions in Canada within a few years. But unemployment has worsened, particularly in the slow-growth regions. In so distorting the economy that corporations can become insensitive to real demand by being cushioned with welfare handouts, the government has laid a foundation for yet more instability. This instability will be paid for not only by the unemployed, but by every individual taxpayer in Canada as long as present policies are pursued. Even now we are reaching the point where taxpayers are virtually bailing out corporations.

In March 1972, the Canadian Manufacturers Association stated that:

> Current improvements [in profitability] have been less than sufficient to stimulate the investment needed or to counteract the alteration in the economics of make-or-buy decisions arising from US investment incentives and Domestic International Sales Corporation (DISC).*

The CMA couldn't miss the golden opportunity of using DISC as a lever to get more favours from government.

The CMA argued that corporate taxes should be reduced to 46 per cent next year rather than three years hence as scheduled, to counteract pressure from the US. Furthermore, the association wanted to see an enlargement of the capital-cost allowance system.

The minister of Finance, the Hon. John Turner, responded with evident enthusiasm in May of this year with a budget that reduced taxes on manufacturing and processing industries to 40 per cent and allows these industries to depreciate their new capital assets over *two years*. The new tax rate of 40 per cent is, however, only the rate that is on the books. With tax concessions, hardly any corporations will ever pay that amount. In previous years, when corporate taxes were 50 per cent on taxable income, many corporations were able to get away with paying minuscule sums in relation to their real earnings.

For example, Imperial Oil Ltd. had net earnings of $1.5 billion from 1965 to 1971. Its income tax over this period

Globe and Mail, March 28, 1972.

was $290 million, representing a rate of 19 per cent. The taxes were this low because Imperial Oil was allowed depreciation and amortization allowances of $394 million and deferred taxes of $85 million. After other deductions and current taxes, the company was left with profits of $709 million.

Shell Canada Ltd. is no less a recipient of welfare assistance. From 1964 to 1969, its net earnings were $516,557,000 —more than half a billion dollars. During that period, Shell Canada paid not one cent of taxes. In 1970, they set aside $16 million for income tax on net earnings of $123 million, a rate of 13 per cent.

Tax breaks and direct grants are the structural components of the corporate welfare state. The tendency to escalate welfare handouts gains momentum with each new failure in the economy. And if fluctuations in the economy proceed in cycles that are increasingly close together, the corporate welfare handouts will remain a permanent feature of our economy. The terrible irony of the permanence of the corporate welfare state is that government incentives to expand capital facilities is a major contributing factor to the boom-bust cycles.

The government depends upon the taxation of individuals, who get no breaks, to support the inequities it perpetrates. The individual is not allowed income-tax deductions such that his taxable income is only a tiny fraction of his net earnings. The individual cannot defer his taxes without paying a penalty. Nor does he receive incentive grants to defray his tax burden.

Because this book deals with two distinct, though related subjects, it is important to make clear at the outset my attitude to each of them respectively.

I oppose in principle the tax concessions and loopholes for which large, often foreign-owned, corporations benefit at the expense of the ordinary Canadian taxpayer. The latter is forced to carry a heavier tax burden because the corporations do not pay their share.

On the other hand, I support the idea of assistance to industry to maintain employment or to create jobs in disadvantaged areas of the country. In this case, my criticism relates to the nature of the programs, their lack of plan and their meagre results.

The two aspects of the corporate welfare system must therefore be kept distinct.

CHAPTER TWO

One City, Two Worlds

Geographers call Sudbury an example of post-glacial topography, but to the Sudbury Chamber of Commerce it is the nickel capital of the world. The post-glacial rocks of the Sudbury basin yield in excess of 20,000,000 tons of ore annually, and through them Canada supplies between 80 and 90 per cent of all nickel in the non-communist world. The demand for nickel is high, and the corporation profits show it.

To the traveller just passing through, the Sudbury landscape is barren, the air is fouled by the acrid stench of sulphur, and the vegetation has been stunted by the endless stream of effluents that spill out of the towering smoke-stacks. But to its 90,000 citizens, Sudbury is home—it is the recipient of their labours and the custodian of their economic survival. In short, it's their living. Proud, hard-working men who come from all parts of the country man the mines and the huge smelters of the International Nickel Company and Falconbridge Mines. (INCO's 16,500 employees represent nearly one-third of the town's total labour force.)

But while Sudbury may provide a living, the living is far from easy for its non-corporate citizens. Many men, unable to find jobs in their home regions and determined not to join the ranks of the permanently unemployed, leave friends and family to respond to the invitation which appears regularly in newspapers across the country, in the form of INCO help-wanted ads to work the mines of the Sudbury basin. Only by suffering severe economic hardship will they be able to have their wives and children join them. Some may never manage it, but settle into the rhythm of mining and smelting life, never easy, but often challenging to courage and skill.

And as surely as workers are the victims of our malfunctioning economy, the corporations are its beneficiaries. The unemployment-creating policies of successive Liberal and Conservative governments provide companies like INCO with a steady and abundant supply of unemployed men to hire—and later discard—at their will.

When work is hard to come by and competition for available jobs is keen, the natural tendency is to take what there is without asking many questions or making many demands. Mining corporations have shown no reluctance in availing themselves of this pressure on labour. However, strong unions and the hard-won recognition that mining involves some of this country's toughest jobs, demanding rugged men with generous measures of stamina and responsibility, have helped to establish incomes that are actually above the national average.

The average income in Sudbury in 1970 was $7530; in that year the basic weekly wage for INCO workers was $138.80. But if the incomes are better than the national average, expenses are worse. Housing costs are among the highest in the country. In 1971 the cost of land had more than doubled over the previous five years, and the average lot was selling for $6490. Single-family dwellings cost an average of $26,580 while the average income of families borrowing money for new homes was $14,248. To look at the situation another way, during 1971 only the combined incomes of two families earning INCO's base wage would have been enough to borrow the money needed for one new home. In addition, severe northern winters result in high heating bills, and food costs reflect the inevitably inflated northern price structure.

In 1970 a realty firm associated with INCO built a series of townhouses on INCO property which rent for $225 per month. Single workers who stay in the company "village," a grouping of trailers outside of Sudbury near the Copper Cliff smelter, receive room and board for $32.55 per week. The only recreational facility is television.

Sudbury faces a problem common to many mining towns. Assets of mining companies are exempt from municipal tax assessments under the Ontario Assessment Act. Municipalities receive payments from the provincial government in lieu of property taxes, but these are usually far from adequate, with the result that the major burden of supplying adequate municipal services falls to the homeowners. The municipality may do its best; the people certainly do their best, but there is not enough money for adequate cultural and recreational facilities, or to repair roads fast enough, or to renovate an older hospital—even to install a sewage-treatment plant.

As might be expected, air pollution is a serious problem. A variety of lung diseases are related to the continuous inhalation of toxic exhaust fumes in mines and smelters. Poor health and even premature death are often the rewards for a lifetime of hard work and service.

Mining is a unique and challenging enterprise, and miners often develop a strange and irresistible attraction to their work. Physically among the most demanding of jobs, the risks and dangers in mining lend it a sense of daring and adventure, but the rewards rarely do justice to the efforts that are required and given. There is a great deal of money in mining, but the men in the mine see little of it—for that we need to go to the corporate executive offices.

The balance sheet of INCO offers an indication of just how much money there really is in mining. The shareholders' equity section of the 1971 statement shows a total of more than one billion dollars, with retained earnings making up $894,969,000 of that.

The 1971 Annual Report indicates that of the 92,217 shareholders, 61 per cent have addresses in Canada, 37 per cent have addresses in the United States, and two per cent elsewhere. Statistics Canada refers to INCO as a Canadian-controlled corporation. However, 49 per cent of the outstanding shares are held by US residents while only 38 per cent are held by Canadians.

INCO production facilities are concentrated in two areas of Canada—Thompson, Manitoba, and Sudbury, Ontario. The Sudbury site includes thirteen mines, four concentrators, a smelter, an iron-ore recovery plant and a refinery.

There is great wealth in our natural resources, but to appreciate it fully one has to leave the town and the mines and head back to the executive suite. Those softly lit, carpeted rooms present quite another picture. There the story is told of how, in 1971, INCO had net earnings of some $210,000,000 and a clear profit of $94,200,000. But when it came time to pay income taxes the government declined. "Don't pay us," they were saying in Ottawa, "We'll pay you!" On a clear profit of $94,200,000 not a single cent was collected in income tax, while the government in 1971 gave INCO a tax *credit* of $2,800,000. By comparison, the non-corporate citizens of Sudbury—you will recall that their average income was $7530 per worker—paid income taxes at the rate of 25 per cent of taxable income.

During the period of 1966 to 1971, the corporation had net earnings of $1,581,000,000 and paid income tax at an effective rate of only 17.2 per cent. Corporation income taxes were kept down by tax deferrals and by special depreciation and depletion allowances. It is interesting to note that while the company deducted $203,300,000 in these allowances, the miners were not even allowed to deduct the $20 they paid out for special shoes to work in the mines. INCO has accumulated deferred income taxes of $238,400,000, representing at best an interest-free loan from the taxpayers and at worst an outright grant. An interest-free loan from the government might be welcomed by INCO workers unable to manage the going interest on mortgages for Sudbury's high-cost housing.

Falconbridge Mines, a second major corporate citizen of Sudbury, provides another interesting comparison with the city's non-corporate citizens. In the years between 1965 and 1971, Falconbridge had an accumulated net income of $211,-000,000—an amount almost the same as the $214,000,000 1970 taxable income of Sudbury's non-corporate citizens. On the same total income, the non-corporate citizens together paid six times as much income tax as Falconbridge Mines did.

The rationalization for the discrepancy is, of course, that the corporation provides jobs, and that reduced taxation will help it to create even more jobs. But INCO, after accumulating deferred income taxes of $238,400,000 and receiving an actual tax credit for the year 1971, laid off 2000 workers in the final six months of that year.

There are *two* worlds in the nickel capital. In the world of the non-corporate citizen, it is a life of hard work, of getting by, of frequent company layoffs. Taxes are deducted at source in most cases and paid by these people as they are assessed. Deferrals, dividends and depletion allowances seem literally worlds away. They are, indeed, worlds away. They can be found only in the realm of the corporate citizen. There, high profits and low taxes are seemingly inseparable companions; depletion allowances and dividends go hand in hand. In the executive suite it is the stench of sulphur and the darkness of a mine shaft that seem worlds away.

In terms of the law as it has been written by Liberal and

15

Conservative governments, INCO obeys the law. It merely takes advantage of the concessions and loopholes which the law provides. So do all the other corporations of which INCO is only one important example.

Reprinted with permission of the *Toronto Star*

Little David

CHAPTER THREE

The Extractive Industries

We Canadians have always taken some pride in viewing ourselves as the fortunate possessors of a large share of the world's mineral wealth. We produce about half the world's nickel, and over 40 per cent of the world's asbestos. We have much more than our share of the world's resources of iron ore, copper, gold, silver, zinc—as well as almost any other mineral. We have the oil and gas of Alberta and promises of immense potential reserves on the Arctic islands and islands off our east and west coasts.

At least, the oil industry and the government are convinced of those reserves in the Arctic, in spite of recent expert testimony before the National Energy Board which raised serious doubts about their extent. Potential reserves, unlike proven reserves, are what the industry expects it may find, not what it has found. This does not alter the basic point that Canada is rich in resources, but it does suggest that perhaps we are not so rich that we can afford to be careless.

We are lucky beyond belief in what we have been given in the way of natural resources. But we are also unfortunate beyond belief in the way in which those resources are squandered. In terms of the advantages we get from them, we are no better off than most banana republics. In fact, we're worse off than some.

The companies that extract our natural resources are largely owned or controlled by the foreign countries that consume them. The oil and gas industry is 74 per cent foreign controlled. The mining and smelting industry is 65 per cent foreign controlled—mainly in the United States.

Thus, we have two major problems rolled into one: the threat to Canadian independence, and the depletion of our resources without matching benefits.

About three-fifths of our metals, gas and oil are exported—again, mainly to the United States—as soon as the primary processing is finished. Foreign tariff legislation and the corporate decisions of multinational firms combine to keep Canadians from turning their own metals into finished products. We extract them mainly so that others can have the benefit of turning them into useful products and exporting them back to us.

This thankless status is partly the result of our relatively small population. A country of twenty-two million people cannot consume the minerals that we are capable of producing. We do not have the range and scale of manufacturing industries to turn into finished products all the metals that our mines produce. We could, with more sensible policies, greatly extend the use of our own minerals and process them in Canada to a stage much nearer the finished product, but we would likely remain exporters of metals, of gas and of oil.

But this is not to say that we have to give those resources away, which is very close to what we are doing. Our mineral companies are gobbling so much from the welfare trough that the net benefits we get from them are much smaller than from any other industry in the country. Why? The prime reason is that our governments have decided that resource industries need not pay their fair share of income taxes.

The oil companies—as they are so fond of pointing out—do collect substantial retail sales taxes from gasoline sales on behalf of governments. But, contrary to their propaganda claims, these taxes are no more taxes on the companies than are the sales taxes that our furniture stores, automobile dealers and other retail outlets collect on behalf of government. These sales taxes are taxes on the consumer, not on the companies or their exports. Consumers would pay them even if Canada produced not one drop of oil or gas.

The only taxes on the companies are the lease fees they pay, royalties, some various minor taxes and the corporate income tax. As it turns out, the corporate income tax is also a minor matter.

How the extractive industries avoid taxes—legally

The process by which a corporation can report its income for income-tax purposes is very different from the process by which it reports those same profits to its shareholders. Both procedures are complex and require the services of expert accountants and tax lawyers.

The profits reported so carefully each year to shareholders are calculated by the firm's accountants on the basis of generally recognized, good accounting principles. The aim of those principles, which apply in different ways to different types of situations, is to provide the fairest statement possible to the shareholders of where the firm stood at the end of the year and how much real profit it made. Those principles are the result of many years of development on the part of the accounting profession. No accountant would contend that they are perfect (indeed, some are the subject of considerable debate in the profession), but they attempt to show the true situation of the company as their accountants and auditors see it.

On that basis, the extractive industries had before-tax profits of $1.13 billion in 1969, the last year for which full statistics are available.

There is, though, a second set of books. And in this second set of books, the mining industry had a "taxable" income of only $136 million in the same year.

Just as the individual Canadian pays tax, not on his gross income but on his taxable income, so does a corporation. In the case of a corporation, however, the deductions made from gross income to arrive at taxable income are vastly more complex (and vastly more generous). They have become so complex that the government has published, in the 1969 edition of *Corporation Taxation Statistics*, a fifteen-page table entitled "Reconciliation of Book Profit to Taxable Income by Major Industry Group."

The mining industry, including gas and oil companies, has been uniquely blessed by government. It has more exemptions than do your car- and fire-insurance policies. In the descent from a 1969 book profit before taxes of $1.13 billion to a "taxable" income of $136 million, there are some thirty-four items to consider, some of them to be added, others to be subtracted.

The four items that bulk largest in making up the difference between what the corporations tell their shareholders and what they tell the tax man are: (1) the exploration and development expenses that are called an investment in Canada's future for publicity purposes and counted as a current expense for income-tax purposes ($569 million); (2) the difference ($160 million) between the depreciation they tell shareholders they incurred and the depreciation the Income Tax Act lets them claim; (3) the depletion allowance ($150 million); and (4) "exempt mine income" ($220 million).

The mining, gas and oil companies will argue, of course, that they should be able to deduct their expenditures on exploration and development from their income before they pay tax on it. And so they should, but not on the basis they do now. To find productive wells, many dry holes must get drilled. As the companies point out, the gushers must pay for the dry holes. Fair enough. But even that reasonable principle has been twisted to produce a tax break for the oil and gas companies.

It is done, as in the case of so many tax breaks, by playing with time and words.

The cost of the dry holes and the cost of the gushers is an investment in producing oil. If you do not spend the money you cannot produce the oil. The logic of that is that the expenditure should be depreciated over the life of the useful assets —the gushers—that are the result of the investment.

The government, however—substantially following the American example—has turned the fact that some holes are dry into an ingenious and very cunning tax give-away.

This is done by pretending that only the investment in gushers is an investment. The necessary investment in holes that turn out to be dry is called a current operating cost. In fact it has obviously nothing to do with current operations. It is no more a current cost than the cost of the hole that turned out to be wet.

But the change in wording means lower taxes. It means that although the investment in the wet holes can be depreciated only over a long period of years for tax purposes, the holes that are dry can be depreciated right away, if it is desirable.

The impact is the same as with accelerated depreciation. The deferred taxes involve the same interest-free loan. But this loan is larger and more valuable because it can be collected in its entirety in the first year. As Statistics Canada puts it, in the 1969 edition of *Corporation Taxation Statistics:*

> *Exploration and development expenses.* Expenditures which under other circumstances might be considered to be of a capital nature are allowable as expenses under certain provisions of the Income Tax Act if such expen-

20

ditures were made by an oil, natural gas or mining company for exploration or development expenses (sec. 83A). The amounts shown here are in addition to those already charged in calculating the company's book profit.

In other words, if it were any other industry, it would receive just ordinary accelerated depreciation. But since it is the mining industry it gets an extra break and can subtract these expenditures immediately. Mining, oil and gas companies write it all off right away in their reports for the government, but not in the reports for their shareholders. Legally.

There is only one reason for the accelerated depreciation and the pretence that oil wells get used up in a year. That reason is to give the industry a tax break. Accelerated depreciation and currently charged exploration and development expenses are a very sneaky way of giving these giant—and largely foreign-controlled—corporations a huge commercial loan from the government and a huge grant at the same time.

Take the simpler case of accelerated depreciation. Suppose a company buys a million dollars' worth of new equipment that will last ten years. The equipment will be used up in producing the gasoline or whatever the commodity is. So accountants, in calculating profit and loss, make a deduction of, say, $100,000 or one-tenth of the value of the equipment in each year of its life. The company's book profits get reduced by that amount each year to allow for the replacement of the equipment when it wears out.

But now a generous government announces that it will let the company claim a capital-cost allowance of, let us say, 40 per cent in each of the first two years and 20 per cent in the third year. Thus the company will have its taxable income reduced by $400,000 in each of the first two years and $200,000 in the third year, rather than the $100,000 that its accountants say represents real depreciation each year.

The effect, with a 50 per cent tax rate, is to reduce the company's taxes by $150,000 each year for two years, and by $50,000 in the third year, for a total of $350,000.

A concrete example of why the industry has learned to stop worrying and love accelerated depreciation is the Alberta Gas Trunk Line Co. That company's annual shareholders' report states that the company has paid no income tax since its inception in 1954 except for $7350 in 1966, even though, from 1964 to 1971 alone, the company cleared profits of $63,000,000.

In later years, of course, the company may pay those deferred taxes, although even this is doubtful. Meanwhile it can use the money as it likes until the time for payment comes, if it ever does.

But when? "When" makes the big difference in the world of corporate finance, just as it does in household finance.

Taxes that you can pay later rather than right now are not just a convenience: they are a huge financial advantage. Of course, the more deductions you have from your income now, the lower your taxes this year. If you use your deductions now, you may still have to pay the taxes later. But paying later is much better than paying now because it amounts to giving you an interest-free loan. While the only interest-free loan that ordinary people can get is the thirty-day credit on furniture purchases, our government gives mining companies interest-free loans on their income taxes that run for years and years.

Accelerated depreciation is really the same thing as getting an automatic, no-questions-asked bank loan at commercial rates, without having to pay any interest. There are many, many individual Canadians who would like to be able to make that kind of arrangement with their government. But the rest of us must pay our taxes when they fall due. We cannot defer them without interest or penalty.

It is a good arrangement for the companies. In the example given above, the interest savings come to nearly $150,000 over the ten years. That $150,000 is a straight gift from taxpayers to the corporation.

The interest-free loan disguised as accelerated depreciation (or the ability to change long-term investments into current expenses) is of course used by the industry. A good part of the income gained from these gifts is used by foreign firms to buy up Canadian companies. And these tax concessions are automatic; they were provided in the tax law before 1971 and they continue to be provided, although in a somewhat softened form, in our new "reformed" tax law.

The same is true of depletion allowances. Until 1977 the government will let mining companies deduct a straight one-third of their income because of depletion. That means quite simply that one-third of their income is absolutely free from tax, forever. Imagine how the ordinary Canadian would benefit from such arrangements.

The theory behind depletion allowances is that a mine or oil well is a depleting resource. So it is. But whose resources are being depleted?

The simple answer is that they are Canada's resources: yours and mine. Not the mining company's resources, for the company generally does not own them. What it has is a right, granted by the federal or provincial government, to take our minerals out of the ground.

It obtains that right by investing money to find our resources, by investing more to extract them and by paying whatever taxes and fees the government decides to get from it. Its investment, which is already written off as exploration costs, is in finding the resources, not in creating them.

The depletion allowance is the ultimate in wrong-way payments. Canada's resources are being exploited and the companies doing the exploiting are provided with a one-third tax reduction into the bargain. Neither the allowance or its name has anything to do with reality except the reality of lower taxes. Nobody, for instance, can offer any explanation of why it should be one-third. That is just a handy amount of tax not to collect.

The new "earned" depletion

Starting in 1977, the old depletion allowance for the extractive industries will be replaced by a new system of earned depletion. Earned depletion means that the deduction of depletion allowances from income will depend on the amount of certain types of expenditures that the company makes. These expenditures are described as eligible expenditures in the amended tax law. For every $3 of eligible expenditures that a company makes, it will be allowed to deduct $1 of earned depletion from its net income.

Those eligible expenditures, however, are already either fully deductible the year they are made or are subject to fast write-offs. With the new change, they will be subtracted from income at the rate of $1\frac{1}{3}$ times. You have yet to hear the worst. During the transition period, companies can continue to claim percentage depletion at 33.3 per cent of net profits, plus earned depletion for the period starting in 1977. All eligible expenditures made after November 7, 1969, earn depletion for the period starting in 1977.

In addition, the three-year tax holiday on income from new mines continues to apply up to December 31, 1973. Of course expenditures to establish new mines are all eligible for accelerated capital-cost allowances.

When all these reforms are added together, not much change is evident, except for the disappearance of the tax holiday.

In most cases it will, given the huge investments projected, be easy to earn the depletion allowance after 1977. The companies that don't earn it can still collect it, if they save up enough eligible expenditures over the next five years—expenditures that they will be able to deduct during these same five years.

Perhaps that explains why they have stopped complaining about tax reform.

How much in taxes is avoided?

The impact of all these concessions is clear from the 1969 taxation statistics, the latest available that show the reconciliation.

In that year, the total taxable income of all 3700 companies in mining, gas and oil was $136 million. If that had been their real income, they would be paying a fair tax. Indeed, there might have been some basis for their continual complaint that their taxes are too high.

But, because of all the corporate sweeteners that a series of Canadian governments have quietly provided at budget time, their taxable income is only a very tiny fraction of their real income.

The difference between the "book profits before taxes" that they proudly report each year to their shareholders in their official annual reports and the taxable income that the government has agreed to tax them on, is bigger than the income difference between the average working man in this country and the president of our biggest bank.

A majority of mining firms, indeed some 80 per cent or more, were able—quite legally—to report in 1969 either that they had no taxable income at all or had shown a loss for tax purposes. At the same time, those losing firms collectively cheered their shareholders with reports of some $400 million in profits.

Some mining companies did, of course, make so much money that even under our tax system they had to pay a fraction of it to the government. Thus some 762 of the 3700 mining companies paid all of the $134 million in taxes that got paid by this sector.

However, this tax-paying minority does not deserve a great deal of sympathy from those of us who see our income taxes carefully deducted from our weekly pay. The fact is that the 762 who had to pay the $134 million in taxes did so on "book profits before taxes" of some $732 million. That is a tax rate of 18 per cent—for those who paid any tax at all.

The collective picture for the industry as a whole is, of course, even more favourable. Total federal and provincial income taxes were the $134 million paid by those who absolutely could not escape them. That is an average rate of only 12 per cent on their book profits.

Oil and gas is even more favoured than the metal mines. The latter pay a tax of 11 per cent while the oil and gas people get away with only 8.6 per cent.

If the mining industry had been paying the full 50 per cent corporate income-tax rate, we would have collected $432 million more in taxes in 1969. That is how much the extractive industries are extracting from us in non-collected income tax every year.

No matter how you add it up, mining companies in Canada have a very sweet deal. Too sweet.

As other parts of this book make clear, the metal-mining, oil and gas industries are not the only ones that benefit from misplaced government generosity. But they do benefit far more than our other industries, as the table below shows.

The taxes that do not get paid by the mining industry must be paid by the rest of us. They are paid by other corporations who are not quite so favoured, and by individual taxpayers. There is no other way.

Percentage of Book Profits* Paid out for Income Tax—1969

Industry	Book profit ($ millions)	Income taxes ($ millions)	% paid
Mines, Gas & Oil Wells	1,132	134	12
Total Manufacturing	3,438	1,377	40
Food	293	119	41
Textile Mills	108	47	43
Clothing	35	15	43
Construction	294	106	36
Retail Trade	480	198	41
All Non-Financial Companies	7,236	2,486	34

SOURCE: Statistics Canada, *Corporation Taxation Statistics* (Ottawa, 1969).

*Book profits before taxes.

Why has government provided these tax breaks?

Canadian governments over the years have provided immensely favoured tax treatment to the mining industry. The basic argument in favour of the assortment of tax breaks that so differentially increase mining profits after taxes, is that they are necessary to provide jobs and to provide export earnings.

The mining industry does provide about one job in every seventy. The total employment in mining, as shown by Statistics Canada for 1969, was 112,490. Like any other industry, the direct jobs support a certain (but unknown) number of indirect jobs in closely related industries that supply services to the mining operations.

The industry also makes a substantial contribution to our exports. Some 60 per cent of our 1969 production of $4.7 billion was exported at the primary processing stage (that is, for labour-intensive fabrication elsewhere) and an additional amount was exported after some fabrication in Canada. The total export value came to $3.9 billion—a little over one-quarter of all Canada's exports of goods.

There can be no question about it. Our mining industry is an important export earner and a relatively small, but nevertheless significant, provider of jobs.

But why should it get tax advantages that are not available to other industries, let alone to individual taxpayers?

The traditional answer to that question is that mining companies can get approximately the same advantages in the United States and other foreign countries. Thus, the argument runs, we must offer just as favourable a tax arrangement if we are to draw them to Canada. That is an argument that sounds plausible. It is, indeed, so plausible that it has convinced literally generations of finance ministers.

It failed, however, to convince the Royal Commission on Taxation, which was appointed by Mr. Diefenbaker and had the misfortune to present its report to the present Liberal government.

Why was the royal commission unimpressed with the traditional argument? Why did it recommend doing away with the vast tax concessions that we still make to the mining industry?

The royal commission started from the basic principle that taxation should be fair. In the famous phrase, "a buck is a buck" no matter who earns it, was the commission's cardinal principle of a good tax system. Its merits are self-evident.

The royal commission worked out the complex mechanics of a fair tax system. It would have provided that mining companies also pay their fair share, after a transitional period to eliminate disruption.

To tax mining companies on a fair basis would not, as the royal commission recognized, result in a decline in their current levels of production, of exports or of employment. It would not make it more expensive for them to extract ore, oil or gas. It would not move any of them from a profit to a loss. All that it would do would be to diminish their after-tax profits. There would be no incentive for them to reduce their activity or their labour force, because if they were to cut production and sales their after-tax profits would also be cut, which would not be in their best interest.

To tax the mining companies fairly, however, would likely involve a slowing-down for a temporary period of exploration and new mine openings in the industry. This would not necessarily be a bad thing at all. Far from being a disadvantage of fair taxation, it would be one of the positive benefits. For the hard fact is that we are being played for suckers by some very smart international corporations and home-grown stock-

27

exchange operators.

Canada is one of the largest storehouses of mineral wealth in the world. That wealth is a fixed amount. It cannot increase. It can only diminish as our rapidly advancing industrial societies gulp more and more raw materials to make the things that our industry produces, to move our cars, to heat our homes, to do all the million and one things that we need metals, oil and gas for.

As the world's population rises, as the demand of the world's people for a fair share of the world's goods rises, the value of raw materials is going to rise. All the studies that have been done forecast increasingly severe raw-material shortages in the United States in the years to come. That country was once a major exporter of oil; it has been an importer for many decades, and will continue to be so despite the recent finds in Alaska. The shortage of natural gas in the United States has grown so substantially that industry sources now talk of tripling the price. Even our own Canadian gas authorities, doubting the industry's inflated estimates of potential reserves, have grown reluctant to authorize further exports to the United States on the grounds that we will need the gas ourselves. The prices of industrial metals have risen sharply over the past decade. There is every reason to expect them to keep on doing so over the long term.

What mining-industry jobs cost—to start

Canada is in the fortunate position of having mineral resources. Why rush to sell now when the price is still low? Ordinary Canadians have no need to do that. The big rush is on the part of the companies who must sell now while income taxes are virtually non-existent.

There might, of course, be a good argument for selling at low prices, if the tax concessions produced a lot of jobs, quickly. Although the tax deal would still be bad long-run policy, it might be justifiable in the short run if we badly needed new jobs, and the concessions made to mining were the best and quickest way to produce them.

We certainly do need more jobs, but the record of the past shows that the mining industry is the most expensive possible way to create a very few of them over a very long period of time.

If you take the period from 1961, a recession year, to 1969 you find that the mining industry increased its employment by about 12,700. The increase would have been a little higher had it not been for strikes.

But during the same period, an investment of some $6.9 billion dollars was required: an investment of the astounding amount of about $540,000 per net new job. In manufacturing, on the other hand, investment over the same period was about $17.0 billion. The extra jobs created amounted to over 340,000. That is $50,000 per extra job, compared with $540,000.

Permanent new jobs in manufacturing do not come cheaply. But they come a lot more cheaply than new jobs in the mining industry.

Imperial Oil is an interesting example. In its latest annual report, it talks—as annual reports normally do—of a generally rosy future. But then it takes note of a little cloud on the horizon:

> One possible source of difficulty could be in attitudes towards resource development. It is now being argued that, for a country like Canada, resource development should be discouraged in favour of manufacturing. The theory is being advanced that only manufacturing can provide the employment opportunities required for Canada's growing labour force, and therefore capital should be channelled into manufacturing facilities rather than extractive facilities.

They are right about the cloud. It is there. They are under it. Although they try to wish the problem away by talking of the very real impact that oil and gas development has had on Alberta in the past, their own annual report is the best possible illustration of the folly of giving gigantic tax subsidies to the extractive industries to boost employment.

What their annual report shows over the last three years is an extra investment of $417 million in capital and exploration expenditures, an increase of more than one-third in after-tax profits and a drop in employment of 497 jobs.

So much for the theory that we can extract jobs from the extractive industries.

Imperial's big project for the next little while is building a new $200-million refinery at Edmonton, which allows it to close refineries in Winnipeg, Regina and Calgary. Imperial Oil evidently anticipates a further employment decline as a result, for they are taking advance steps to find suitable employment for those to whom they cannot offer jobs in Edmonton and for those who are not ready to retire.

Imperial Oil is not consciously a bad company or a bad employer. The new refinery, for instance, is at least partly designed to control its own pollution. The corporation is simply responding to the massive bias built into our tax system. That system makes it very profitable to invest in new plants. It makes it not at all profitable to invest in people. It is, in a very real and profound sense, a tax system with a massive bias against the people of Canada who want a steady job.

But that is only half the story. The figures show only the amounts that the mining industry—and the people of Canada through corporate tax concessions—must invest to create new jobs. They overlook the immense outlays needed by provincial and municipal governments and, from time to time, the federal government.

New mines almost always open in the less-populated areas of the country. Sometimes a new mine will open beside an old one. But more frequently it will be in a remote area, removed from existing highway and rail networks, and in a place where there are no schools, hospitals, sewers or any of the other amenities of urban life.

For example, Cominco recently opened a huge strip-mining operation at Pine Point near Hay River in the Northwest Territories. To serve this new mine and others in the far North, the federal government built a railway from Alberta to Hay River at a cost of $86 million. The federal government also built an all-weather road and a rail spur from Hay River to Pine Point, as well as a $9-million power plant. These expenditures will benefit others in the North, but the biggest benefactors, at least in the immediate future, are the people who get the dividends from Cominco.

All these things cost money. We have to pay for them through provincial sales taxes, through the real-estate tax and, indirectly, through payments and grants that the federal government makes to the provinces.

We also pay in other ways. The huge amounts of borrowing needed put stress on capital markets. That pushes up interest rates, including those on home mortgages. The high interest rates attract foreign capital flows, which push up our exchange rates. The rise in the exchange rate makes our manufactured exports more expensive on world markets, and thus holds down new job creation in the manufacturing industry. We suffer in indirect ways from the irrational preference that Mr. Turner and his Liberal and Conservative predecessors have had for the mining industry.

The hidden burdens are very real. Statistics Canada does not add them up, so we cannot tell how much extra the small increase in mining jobs has actually cost us over the last ten years.

An expanding population will, of course, require investment in municipal services even if no new mines are opened. But the expense of building new roads, railways, ports or air facilities is avoided when development occurs in or near the towns and cities where people already live. The cost to government— to you and me—of the services required for 1000 jobs in Prince Rupert, in Regina, in Winnipeg, in Thunder Bay or in Bathurst is much lower than when a new mine is opened fifty or one hundred miles from a road.

What mining-industry jobs cost—when the ore runs out

The opening of a new mine site miles from existing roads or towns has traditionally been a cause for rejoicing. Even if it happens more and more rarely it is still welcome, particularly in these times of high unemployment.

But there is another, rather tarnished, side to the coin. It has been apparent since the end of the Second World War in northern Ontario, in Quebec, in the Atlantic provinces and even in the newer mining areas of the West. Every mine that opens will, some day, close. When the ore is gone and the profits have been taken out, the whistle will blow for the last time.

The people, the miners, will still be there. After years or decades of heavy toil they will have nothing but houses, in a town that has died with the mine that created it.

Their alternatives will be few. You cannot sell a house in a town where everybody is leaving and nobody is settling. You cannot get a new job there, either. If you are over fifty, all you can do is watch the younger, unattached men and women leave, while you collect what is left of your unemployment-insurance cheques and wait until you reach sixty-five and become eligible for your government pension. If you are young enough, and well-educated enough, and willing to abandon the life savings that you have put into your house, you can close the door behind you and try your luck at another mining job in another mining town.

The opening of a new mine is a joyous occasion; its inevitable closing is a social and economic tragedy.

The mining-company executives jet away and leave the government to pick up the pieces. They have taken their tax-free profits. They leave the municipal debts to their workers.

Some companies keep on paying pensions to the miners who earned them when the mine was working. Others just siphon out the profits and fold up the company.

The examples provided by the gold mines in Ontario and Quebec and the coalfields in Nova Scotia are instructive. They foretell the inevitable future of other mining areas.

In 1948 the government of Canada realized that time was running out for the gold mines in Ontario and Quebec. Most mines, some of them in operation for decades, were being forced to operate on lower- and lower-grade ore. The once-rich veins yielded less and less. With the need to attract and keep labour by paying at least moderate wages, company costs were rising.

The price of gold, on the other hand, was fixed at $35 an ounce. Costs were rising, but prices were set by the determination of the United States Treasury not to pay more for gold.

The operators appealed to Ottawa. They told the government that they would need subsidies to keep their mines open. They pointed out, correctly, that the economic and social consequences of widespread closures would be horrendous. They pointed out, again correctly, that gold sales earned foreign exchange.

They got their subsidy. So far, from 1948 to 1971, it has cost us $289 million in "emergency gold-mining assistance." In 1970 only one of our remaining twenty-eight gold mines was not on the dole.

Despite that aid—much of which goes to fatten the profits of the mining companies—the gold-mining industry has declined rapidly. Until the recent increases in the world price of gold, the normal pattern was for several mines to close each year, leaving some hundreds or thousands of long-term employees wondering how they were going to survive.

The same pattern showed up in the case of the coal mines of Cape Breton. In one form or another Canadian governments have been giving handouts to coal companies since 1927. Until recently, the handout was mostly in the form of the "transportation subsidy" for coal. That subsidy was used to make Cape Breton coal cheaper in central Canada. It was also used to a lesser degree to make coal from Alberta and British Columbia cheaper in central Canada and in Japan.

The argument was that our domestic coal was situated too far from central Canadian markets. In Ontario it could not compete with foreign coal nor with heating oil. As the Cape Breton mineshafts were pushed more and more miles out under the sea, the operators argued that the government must subsidize them or face massive unemployment in Cape Breton.

Once again, the argument was correct. Once a mine is there and people are working in it, they are dependent on it. As seams run out and costs rise, the subsidies must also rise. If they do not, the companies will not have an adequate profit and will pull out. Government must step in to help resolve the problems.

The subsidies rose. They rose to the point where the miners' wages were being paid for largely by the subsidies, rather than by the coal the miners produced.

The coal companies, now living on the subsidies, stopped caring. They did not make the necessary investments in modernization.

Eventually, they got out. Over the years it had cost the federal government alone some $320-odd million to keep the coal mines going. By 1968, even the government had begun to realize that there was a crisis.

For once it did something that was, in concept, sensible and humane. It created a crown corporation, DEVCO, to take over the dying mines. It decided to pay the pensions that Hawker-Siddeley said it could not pay. And it began to put money into industrial development.

That effort has involved considerable government expense, both in the modernization that the companies had not undertaken and in industrial-development funds. It is costing us some $42 million this year alone; that is the current part of our bill for cleaning up after Hawker-Siddeley. And it has yet to pay off. DEVCO has been reorganized after its initial adventures. Its success is very doubtful, but even if DEVCO has little more success in the future than it has had in the past, it will be recognized as an attempt to do the right thing for a change.

There has still been no crown corporation established to bring new industry to the mining towns of Ontario and Quebec that have been hit by the closing of gold mines. The federal government has been unable to think of anything better than to continue subsidizing the mining companies and offering the odd "regional-development" grant. It has not even been helping the miners and their families with some form of pension, as in the case of the coal miners. The gold miners have been too undemanding.

The saddest part of the depressing story of mine closures is that, despite the immense sums involved, the federal government has paid only a fraction of the cost involved in picking up after the mining companies. The mining companies have paid nothing.

Most of the cost is paid by the individuals who lose out and by the towns they live in. The government has done nothing to prolong the life of mines other than those which produce coal or gold. It has responded to the needs of the people left behind only when it could not escape the political consequences. Many mines, in all parts of the country, close and leave problems. The people and the towns are left to fend for themselves because these are "individual" or "local" problems; they are not "industry-wide" problems. They no longer have an industry lobby which could use them as an excuse to wring profit-increasing subsidies out of the government, because the industry has left.

The corporate liberal defence

Recently, the corporate establishment has begun to react to the growing discontent shown by Canadians with the fact that our highly profitable extractive industries do not pay their fair share of taxes.

The reaction is based on the tactic the Liberals generally use when faced with their shortcomings: if you can't convince people, scare hell out of them.

When the prime minister announced that he was going to

"stop inflation dead" by permitting unemployment to rise to 6 per cent if necessary, he was telling the country, in effect, that some people would have to lose their jobs in order to prevent inflation from running wild. Moreover, if Canadians weren't prepared to make sacrifices, they deserved chaos.

The beauty of this favourite Liberal ploy lies in the simplicity of its logic: either accept my solution or face greater disaster. The logic becomes particularly compelling when one reflects that, since the government has the power to force its "solution" on the country, the "greater" disaster is never seen. A callous debating trick arouses people's fears of the "greater" disaster, but no proof of its inevitability is ever offered, because it can't be proven. The need either to justify a policy or to discuss the alternatives to that policy rationally is avoided.

In such a manner does the favourite tactic of the Trudeau government operate. Precisely the same device is now being used by those who profit from the non-payment of corporate income taxes, and by those who have to justify their past mistakes in providing such tax breaks.

We can expect to see a great deal of this kind of nonsense in the 1972 electoral campaign. It has already started.

The minister of Finance, John Turner, for example, has recently been testing out the corporate version of the big scare. In a recent trip to northern Ontario, in front of a nomination meeting for a local Liberal, he did his level best to frighten the wits out of the people of Timmins. As reported by the Canadian Press, he said:

> Mr. Lewis would turn this town into a ghost town if he implemented his policies. If Mr. Lewis had his way, all the residents of Timmins would be trapping, fishing, hunting or living in southern Ontario.

The people of Timmins, after hearing those words, were supposed to march right out and vote Liberal to save their skins. It is the same old business of "Accept my policy or my opponent will ruin you utterly."

Mr. Turner, of course, does not carry off the big scare very well. He is still inexperienced. He makes his fictional disasters too big and too immediate to be convincing. It is just too much to suppose that the people of Timmins will all be living on whatever rabbits they can catch on the morning after the election.

People are no longer very vulnerable to these tactics. They are not likely to be convinced that the Timmins mining companies' use of untaxed profits to buy shares of companies operating elsewhere in Canada or in the United States makes jobs in Timmins. They are not likely to be convinced that depletion allowances keep mines from becoming depleted or companies from giving mines up as the seams of ore narrow down and peter out.

They do see, as have so many tens of thousands of people in northern Ontario and Quebec, how the government must now pay to keep mines alive and people working because the huge profits of the fat years were not taxed.

They see and they wonder. They are not the fools that Mr. Turner takes them for. The people of Canada are not little children who scurry to bed when the Liberal bogeyman comes by. He has been coming too often.

The Liberals are, however, not alone in their defence of the extractive industries.

As pitiful as the recent income-tax reform proposals were, the Tories stridently opposed even those reforms. Progressive Conservative finance critic Marcel Lambert opposed the legislation as "a system of legalized plunder and piracy by people motivated by desire for the have-nots to take from the haves." He criticized the capital-gains tax, on the grounds of that famous bogeyman of the Conservatives, uncertainty in the business sector.

Mr. Lambert, like other Tories and Liberals, is a champion of that oppressed underdog, the mining industry in Canada. Speaking in Parliament on May 11, 1972, he said:

> With respect to the mining industry, I would like to ask whether the Minister has read the recent speeches by the president of the Mining Association of Canada. Has he read the annual report by the president of Noranda? I hope he takes it to heart . . . I commend it to all members.

What would a rational policy be?

A rational national policy towards the mining industry should be high on our list of priorities.

The essence of that policy should be fair treatment of the operators of our mines, gas and oil wells. Profits from these operations—despite their extractive nature—should be treated and taxed on the same basis as the profits of our other corporations. There is no reason to go on subsidizing the running down of our resources by maintaining mining corporations as the favoured darlings of the tax rip-off system. That must end.

We must, though, not merely insist that they pay their taxes. We must require them to set aside, during the fat years, the funds to ease the exceptional human and economic problems they will inevitably leave behind when they have run out of ore. There is no reason why their workers and the taxpayers should be the ones to suffer. What we need is a fair tax arrangement sufficient to build up a fund to pay for early retirement benefits, retraining and mobility grants, the losses workers must take on their homes and the losses the towns must take on their bonds.

If the combination of these two things were to slow down the opening of new mines for a while, that would be entirely a good thing. Our investment priorities have been distorted by the tax system. They desperately need a new direction.

If we present the bill to the corporations they will pay. They certainly have the money. But we cannot even present the bill if we have governments that must rely—as Mr. Trudeau and Mr. Stanfield do—on the campaign contributions of the firms themselves.

It is as simple as that. Welfare is for the needy, not big and wealthy multinational corporations.

CHAPTER FOUR

The Land Envelopers

Most housing built in the next decade will probably be constructed on land already owned by one of a few large builder-developers who have come to control land markets in recent years. The recently released Dennis report,* which presents the findings and recommendations of a Central Mortgage and Housing Corporation study group commissioned to advise the government on policies for low-income families and individuals, shows the extent of monopolistic and oligopolistic land holdings in Canadian cities.

Residential Land Demand and Supply
1971–1980

City	CMHC estimates of 10-year requirements	Acreage controlled by six leading developers
Calgary	7,500	7,500
Edmonton	8,790	8,500
Halifax	2,250	1,600
London	4,252	3,820
Montreal	12,000	3,000
Ottawa-Hull	8,128	7,000
Toronto	19,600	18,000
Vancouver	8,000	6,900
Victoria	4,571	nil
Winnipeg	8,000	6,155
Windsor	3,000	1,500
Regina	1,250	1,250

SOURCE: Dennis and Fish, *Low-Income Housing,* p. 604.

Many ordinary Canadians will be surprised by the extent of market concentration. The figures in the above table are only an indication of the degree of monopoly and oligopoly control that exists. The holdings of a number of other large companies

*Michael Dennis and Susan A. Fish, *Low-Income Housing: Programs in Search of a Policy,* draft report for CMHC (Ottawa, April 1972).

are not shown, since these companies are not among the largest six in a given community.

Land developers also have many ways of controlling local land stocks. Their land options do not appear in this table; nor does land held in trust for the developer or held in other corporate names, many of which are difficult to trace. What the table does show is that at most, six land developers control the land markets in many Canadian cities. If you move to a new home in the next decade, it will likely be built on their land, which they will sell at vastly inflated prices.

Which are the corporations that control such vast amounts of urban land? In Toronto, three firms own in excess of 5000 acres each: Bramalea Development Corporation, Canadian Equity and Development Corporation and S. B. McLaughlin Associates Ltd. Canadian Equity, which owns Don Mills development and the Erin Mills New Town, is controlled by the Cadillac Development Corporation and by the Bronfman (Seagram's) interests. A large shareholder in Bramalea is Eagle Star Insurance, which also holds an interest in another large developer: Trizec Corporation.

Other large land holders in the Toronto area are George Wimpey (Canada) Limited, Monarch Construction Limited and Richard Costain (Canada) Limited. All are wholly owned subsidiaries of British building companies. Another is Markborough Properties Limited, among whose major stockholders are George Wimpey and the Royal Bank. Kaufman and Broad Inc., a major American developer, recently acquired the prime land-holdings of Revenue Properties Limited, by having acquired all the shares of its subsidiary, the Victoria Wood Development Corporation.

The Canadian land market is among the most lucrative in the world, and greater profits are made in the Toronto market than anywhere else in Canada. Lot prices for single-family houses average $13,000 and the land costs comprise 36 per cent of the price of an NHA-financed bungalow.* Concentration is as extensive in other cities. Headway Corporation supplies most of the land developments in Thunder Bay, while LADCO is the largest landholder in Brandon. On the prairies, Genstar Limited, the Canadian subsidiary of a Belgian con-

*Andrezej Derkowski, *Inelasticity of Supply in the Toronto Housing Market*, unpublished MA thesis, University of Toronto, 1971.

glomerate, has acquired control of BACM Construction and Materials Limited. BACM owns over 2500 acres (one-third of the requirements for the next ten years) in Winnipeg alone, and is one of the major land developers in Edmonton. One of Edmonton's other major developers is Western Realty Projects Limited, which obtains a major share of its funds from its equity shareholder, City Savings and Trust, Edmonton. Western Realty has also expanded into Vancouver and is reportedly seeking development sites in Toronto.

Large-scale private land assembly by land developers is a recent phenomenon in Vancouver. On May 1, 1971, the president of Western Realty announced in the *Vancouver Sun* that his company acquired a ten- to fifteen-year land bank in the area. Marathon Realty Limited, a wholly owned subsidiary of Canadian Pacific Railways, is a major developer. Other major developers in Vancouver include Dawson Developments Limited, Imperial Construction Limited and Intercontinental Construction.

It should be borne in mind that the estimates of land holdings in the Dennis report are not always accurate. The CMHC information officer in Vancouver admitted that the survey of land holdings in that city was conducted over the telephone by an appraiser. Some of the information is now out of date, but some of the developers who reacted to the report were kind enough to provide the nation with a more accurate accounting.* Western Realty claimed it owned 975 acres while Dawson Developments said it owned 697 acres in the greater Vancouver area.

In his report, Mr. Dennis stressed that:

> . . . the concentration of landholding in a small number of very powerful holders is a new phenomenon. A small number of firms can now decide the pace at which land will be serviced.**

This situation is reason enough for the ordinary Canadian to be concerned about the ownership of his urban future. There are two additional reasons. First, increases in the cost of housing are a major component of the huge inflation which

---

*James Spears and Gary Bannerman, "Critics Roast Housing Report," *Vancouver Province*, August 18, 1972.

**p. 606.

Mr. Trudeau's Liberal government has fostered; a close examination of this increase in housing costs reveals that the cost of land is a major contributor to it. The following table provides a ten-year comparison between the escalation in land costs and housing-construction costs and the cost increases of all other consumer items. The cost of land has increased almost 2.5 times as fast as other consumer items.

Price Indexes, 1961–1971

Year	Land costs[1] NHA dwellings	Construction cost[1] per square foot NHA dwellings	All[2] items
1961	100.0	100.0	100.0
1962	107.0	98.3	101.2
1963	114.3	99.0	103.0
1964	118.4	103.1	104.8
1965	118.9	109.3	107.4
1966	133.7	117.7	111.4
1967	137.6	122.9	115.4
1968	144.0	130.5	120.1
1969	161.5	139.8	125.5
1970	194.5	143.0	129.7
1971	187.8	147.9	136.3

1. SOURCE: CMHC, *Canadian Housing Statistics, 1971* (Ottawa, 1972), table 112.
2. SOURCE: Statistics Canada, *Prices and Price Indexes* (Ottawa, 1971).

Moreover, as the Dennis report emphasizes, the impact of these galloping land prices does not fall only on the new home buyers. They affect the price of all housing:

> On the basis of the evidence . . . we conclude that the cost of new houses is a major influence on the prices of houses in general. This is a remarkable observation. The number of single detached dwellings produced in a year in Canada is currently about 75,000. The number of MLS (Multiple Listing Service) transactions per year in Canada is also about 75,000. The total stock of single detached dwellings in Canada is about 3.5 million. Yet the prices of new houses dominate the market for all houses.*

*p. 16-17.

The second reason why the ordinary Canadian taxpayer should be concerned about these findings—alarmed would be a better word—is that successive federal governments have fostered these developments by their unending subsidies through the tax system and through direct government grants over the past twenty-five years. Most of the firms mentioned above have been the recipients of major government handouts, euphemistically called "tax deferrals." They are an example of corporate welfare since they have been provided loopholes that put them in a lower tax bracket than most ordinary Canadian taxpayers. As is the case in other sectors of the corporate welfare state, these handouts amount to tens of millions of dollars. Let us look at how the system works.

First, examine the handouts which are given through the operations of the taxation system. Land developers benefit in two ways. On the one hand, the cost of holding land for development is tax deductible, including the interest payments on the money which is borrowed to buy the land. An individual taxpayer could not deduct these interest payments from taxable income. The Liberal government's 1971 amendments to the Income Tax Act closed this loophole for individuals:

> The carrying charges on undeveloped real property (e.g., vacant land) will not be deductible from other income in situations where the property is being held as a capital investment.*

However, the change did not apply to large corporations. Land is not a capital investment for them; it is a business. The land developers lobbied hard to prevent the loss of this loophole. Major firms, as well as the Canadian Institute of Public Real Estate Companies and the Urban Development Institute, presented briefs to the Finance minister emphasizing the adverse impact of these proposals. Actually, the links between land developers and the government are closer than that. Members of the Housing and Urban Development Association of Canada (HUDAC) meet regularly in pre-arranged sessions with the management of CMHC. They are the only interest group formally accorded this privilege.

In spite of government claims of tax reform, the large land-

---

*Canada Department of Finance, *Summary of 1971 Tax Reform Legislation* (Ottawa, 1971), p. 51.

development corporations have retained their loophole.

It is often said that closing tax loopholes such as this would result in higher prices, in this case in higher land prices. This suggests that the existence of loopholes contributes in some way to keeping land prices down. In fact land developers take advantage of both the tax concession to reduce their taxes *and* their customers to add to their profits.

Developers can still deduct the cost of holding land from their gross income. Interest payments on their mortgages, municipal taxes and so one are considered business.

The cost of holding land for future use is also a deductible expense. Interest payments on mortgages, municipal taxes and so on are deductible for tax purposes, but the developers add these same expenditures to the cost of the land they sell.

The 1971 annual report of Richard Costain (Canada) Ltd. explains it quite clearly:

> Carrying charges (interest and real-estates taxes), and an appropriate portion of the salaries and expenses of personnel directly related to development are added to the cost of lands and work in progress, and for the current year such additions, net, amounted to $695,792 (1970: $495,790).

Charges deducted from gross income for tax purposes are added to the price the homebuyer pays. The tax loophole does not result in a lower price for the buyer of a Costain dream home; it results in higher profits for the company.

Other charges are also added to the price of land to the buyer, or the rent of the renter. The difference between the cost of the land to the company and the value it is appraised at later becomes part of the company's profits and part of the price paid by the homebuyer. Frequently the company is able to avoid tax on this amount, and the amounts are often considerable.

The 1971 annual report of the Nu-West Development Corporation, which operates principally in Calgary, Edmonton and Vancouver, explains it to the shareholders of the company:

> Based on appraisals made as at December 31, 1971, land held by the company with a book value of $7,372,620 had an appraised value of $11,763,968, for an appraisal surplus of $4,391,348. In addition, the

company's proportional share of the land held by non-controlled corporate joint ventures with a book value of $3,215,855 was appraised at a value of $8,166,117, for a surplus of $4,950,262.

The total difference, or "appraisal surplus," is $9,341,610.

Paper losses resulting from interest payments and excess depreciation (or accelerated capital-cost allowance, if you want the government euphemism) are other tax handouts that work for the land developers just as they do for other corporations. However, since housing is so capital intensive, the gains for the real-estate giants are particularly large. Such generosity on the part of government has led to the oligopolistic tendencies which have recently developed in this industry. Capital goes where the biggest profits are to be had. With the liberal tax benefits available, it is little wonder land development and real estate are attractive. An investment in real estate can be recovered tax free by depreciation deductions; they recover more than 40 per cent of the cost in the first quarter of the useful life of the investment, even though actual depreciation usually increases directly with the age of the building.

Moreover, the real-estate developer does not depreciate only his equity in the development. He deducts the entire building cost, including the part financed by a mortgage. For example, if a developer's equity is 20 per cent of the building cost, accelerated tax depreciation over the first quarter of the building's life will be twice his initial investment. The extent to which this feature has contributed to the growth of oligopoly in the industry cannot be overstated. Ownership of a building may generate a tax-free cash flow which can be used to purchase more real estate. As a consequence, many of today's large real-estate developers owe much of their success and growth to these generous features of the income-tax legislation. The Dennis report arrived at the same conclusion:

> For professional developers, the apparent liability to tax on land profits is offset by the deductions allowed by the legislation. Land developers can deduct from other income the property taxes, interest and other carrying costs of land held as inventory for future development, and paper losses resulting from interest payments and depreciations of rental buildings. The effect, in the case of large corporations, is an interest-

free loan from the government of 52 per cent of the tax otherwise payable, to be used for the acquisition of more land. Under section 18 of Bill C-259 [the revised Income Tax Act] this write-off is not available to people who are not in the land-development business, . . . but is retained for professional developers.*

In the end it is not government which is giving this interest-free loan to real-estate operations, but the Canadian taxpayer. This is an interest-free loan to "free" enterprises to increase capital acquisition. The government cannot claim that housing would not be built if it were not for these subsidies. Nor do the subsidies reduce rents, since the benefits gained by the developer are not passed on to the consumer. Nor, in fact, can these benefits be called subsidies: they are nothing less than blatant handouts.

The present concentration of land ownership, as well as concentration in other sectors, is a direct result of a tax system developed by successive Liberal and Tory governments. It is a system that is wrong. Even the corporations admit that buildings do not depreciate as rapidly as the government permits. For instance, the 1971 annual report of the Cadillac Development Corporation had this to say about depreciation:

The company records depreciation on buildings included in income-producing properties on a 5 per cent, fifty-year straight-line basis. Under this method, depreciation is charged to income in an amount which increases annually consisting of a fixed annual sum together with interest compounded at the rate of 5 per cent per annum so as to fully depreciate the buildings over a fifty-year period.

Moreover, the same firm also insists that it is its cash flow, rather than profits recorded for tax purposes, which reflects the true financial position of the company:

We believe that, in measuring financial performance in the real-estate industry, cash flow is as important a gauge as net income. Cash flow is the sum of net income, depreciation, deferred income tax and other non-cash charges . . . The cash-flow figure indicates the amount of funds available to meet company obliga-

*p. 612.

tions, including mortgage principal repayments, *and the amount of internal funds generated for growth.*

This is indeed the mechanism for capital acquisition and growth, a mechanism which is running wild.

Yet when this matter is raised, those who have propagated the system and those who have the most to gain by its continuation try to confuse the issue by making international comparisons, particularly to Sweden and the alleged fact that corporation taxes there are much lower than ours. They do not go on to examine the rest of the Swedish income-tax structure. The Swedish system is much more progressive than ours; income is much more equitably distributed, and capital-cost allowances are much less than our own: 0.6 per cent per annum for stone apartment houses, increasing to only 3 – 5 per cent for wooden buildings.* Canadian corporations can depreciate stone or brick apartment houses at a rate eight times faster than in Sweden; frame buildings can be depreciated at 10 per cent per annum, a rate twice as fast as Sweden's.

If international comparisons are to be made, then the country whose tax legislation most clearly approximates Canada's today is the United States of America. The derelict buildings and the physical and human desolation afflicting the inner cities of that country's largest communities are in large part a legacy of government neglecting its responsibility to its citizens. Can we expect the same conditions for our major cities in the years to come?

The rules by which the corporate land developers play the game have been described. Let us now turn to the players.

Cadillac Development Corporation Ltd.

Cadillac owns over 5000 acres in Metropolitan Toronto. It has a 40 per cent interest in Canadian Equity and is responsible for managing the Erin Mills New Town development. In addition, it controls entirely or in part some 13,200 residential dwelling units (December 31, 1971).

Cadillac has had net earnings from 1966 through 1971 of approximately $62,968,000. Since Cadillac has been more adept at utilizing the loopholes provided in Canada's tax laws than

---

*Robert W. Davis, *Capital Cost Allowances,* Studies of the Royal Commission on Taxation, Number 21 (Ottawa, 1966), p. 227.

most other companies, they paid during this period a total of $20,506 in taxes, an infinitesimal amount. The percentage is not even worth computing. If this book had been written one year ago, it could have been reported that Cadillac had paid no income taxes whatsoever.

Cadillac has perfected the art of playing the tax game. Moreover, its records show the extent of the excessive capital-cost allowance. The company claims that its total depreciation for 1966–1971 was $4,986,000, yet it has accrued deferred taxes in just four of these years to the extent of $8,879,000. Since the tax rate is nearly 50 per cent, this figure indicates that Cadillac's total capital-cost allowance deductible for purposes of income taxation has been nearly $18 million, nearly four times what it is in Cadillac's own records.

In the same period, 1966–1971, Cadillac's assets have increased nearly threefold, from $96,200,000 to $272,194,000.

Canadian Equity and Development Company Ltd.

Canadian Equity and Development Ltd. is owned by the Cadillac and Bronfman interests. It owns over 5000 acres in metropolitan Toronto and is a major source of land for Cadillac. The company has paid taxes, but it is becoming more adept at the tax loophole game, probably following the example of its proud parent, Cadillac. In 1966, net income was 50 per cent of cash flow. In 1971, the percentage was 37. Research also reveals that an increasing proportion of Canadian Equity's net profits has sales of land as its source: net profits have increased from 29 per cent to 51 per cent of its total net income.

Revenue Properties Ltd.

The history of Revenue Properties Ltd., majority stockholders in Century City Developments Ltd. (an aborted new "developed" town in Uxbridge and Pickering townships northeast of Toronto) is a stormy one. However, it may end on a happy note —for Revenue Properties Ltd., that is. The Department of Transport is proposing to build the new Toronto airport on land owned by Century City. 1600 acres of the 6600 acres reserved for Century City are being considered for expropriation. Development of an additional 3500 acres of the remaining 5000 is being reserved, pending possible regulations that may limit the intensity of development. Unless there is a drastic re-ordering of priorities, the local authorities and the federal and provincial governments will permit as much development as possible. (There has been a previous example. The development of land controlled by Bramalea Developments encroached on the existing facility at Malton airport in Toronto, which eventually resulted in the necessity to find a new air-terminal site.) In any event, it can be taken for granted that the new town the Ontario government says it will build will increase Century City's property values and thus bail them and their major shareholders out of the financial difficulties which they have experienced in the past few years.

The 6600 acres of Century City are carried on its books at a value of $12,673,000. Revenue Properties owns additional land which it carries on its books at $15,105,000. Of course it is able to deduct the carrying charges from income and thus show an operating loss for taxation purposes.

We cannot discern the precise level of welfare payments to this company because in writing their 1970 financial statements in May of this year, their auditors felt compelled to note that:

> Because of the significance of the matters set out in the preceding paragraphs and the substantial amounts which may be involved, we are unable to express an opinion as to whether the consolidated financial statements, taken as a whole, present fairly the financial position of the company as at December 31, 1970... As required by the Business Corporations Act we report that the accompanying consolidated financial statements do not fulfil the requirements of the Act concerning financial statements.

There was no question as to whether or not the financial statement, issued by Revenue Properties in its 1968 annual report, presented fairly the financial position of the company. Revenue Properties was convicted of issuing a false financial statement.

With the ordinary welfare recipient, the welfare agency sends around a case worker to determine his true financial status. If he has not reported his affairs accurately he is dropped from the dole. But we treat our corporate recipients

48

more gently. This one, Revenue Properties, will reap the benefits of having the government locate an air-terminal in its backyard.

Markborough Properties Ltd.

Markborough Properties is developing 3000 acres north of Toronto in the Mississauga-Streetsville area, to be known as Meadowvale. In addition, the company is planning a residential development in Agincourt North to be called either Brimley Wood or Brimley Forest. (The annual report refers to both.)

Markborough did not pay one cent in income tax to the federal and provincial governments between 1966 and 1970. During this time the company's net earnings were $12.1 million.

Why? First, the company was able to charge $1.7 million in depreciation against net earnings as well as $200,000 in bank interest and $5.0 million in mortgage interest. The average non-corporate taxpayer has to pay tax on his mortgage payments; corporations do not.

What remains of the $12.1 million, after deducting $5.0 million in mortgage interest, $0.2 million in bank interest and $1.7 million in depreciation, is $5.2 million. Of this, $2.7 million was deferred tax and $2.5 million was profits. The amount of tax paid in the five years was nil.

In the words of the 1971 annual report of the company:

> In calculating taxable income the company avails itself of certain provisions of the Income Tax Act to eliminate taxes currently payable, and, as a result, all provisions for income tax to date are shown in the balance sheet as deferred income taxes. Based on the company's projections of future taxable income, no portion of the deferred tax liability will be payable before 1976.

The report proudly relates that:

> The Ontario Government announced further details of its "Toronto-Centred Regional Plan" during the year. The plan acknowledges Meadowvale and environs as a major growth centre.

Those who argue that the system has been reformed should note that the interim statement for the first six months of 1972 shows $764,000 in deferred taxes, compared to $24,000 in the first six months of 1971.

BACM

BACM is likely the largest land developer in the four western provinces. Over 99 per cent of its stock is owned by Genstar Ltd. It is, for all practical purposes, a wholly owned subsidiary. Genstar, in turn, is sponsored by Société Générale de Belgique. BACM is a model of vertical integration. It owns Standard Holdings Ltd., Jefferies Developments Ltd. of Calgary, Redi-Mix Ltd. of Saskatchewan, Con Force Products Ltd. of Saskatchewan, Alberta Holdings and Rex Holdings of Alberta, Universal Construction Co. Ltd. of Calgary, Universal Builders' Supplies Ltd., Engineered Buildings Ltd., Preco Concrete Products Ltd., Dartmouth Developers Ltd. and Keith Construction Co. of Winnipeg.

As of December 31, 1971, the company held land for sale valued at $32,218,000, land located in every major western city. This represents 11,400 acres; over 2000 acres are in metropolitan Winnipeg.

In 1968, building materials, heavy construction, land development and housing comprised 26 per cent of Genstar's revenues and 22 per cent of its net income. By 1971, the figures had become, respectively, 54 per cent and 55 per cent. Genstar's rate of taxation, at 18.1 per cent in the period 1966–1971, was higher than many other companies. But in this period it had deferred tax payments of $8,199,000, more than enough to pay the interest on its $32-million worth of land. Like other land developers, it received an interest-free loan to acquire land and other assets. Of course the ordinary taxpayers have to pick up the tab for these handouts. There is also the fact that should one of these taxpayers buy land from BACM–Genstar (and in some cities he would have very little choice if he wanted a home there), he can expect to pay interest on his own mortgage, interest which is not tax deductible.

Canada Interurban Properties Ltd.

Canada Interurban Properties Ltd. is another company that has paid no income tax. From 1966 to 1970 it had net earnings of $31,563,048. It deferred $4,979,500 in taxes in those five years; it has in fact accrued over $6 million in deferred taxes since it was acquired by Power Corporation in 1963. It owns shopping centres, office buildings and townhouses in Ottawa and Montreal. Through its wholly owned subsidiary, William Teron Ltd., it is involved in the development of 3200 acres in the Ottawa area developmental town of Kanata and owns 737 acres in Mount Bruno, Quebec.

Nu-West Corporation Ltd.

Nu-West Corporation's present structure and activities provide an excellent example of the effects of our present tax system. Nu-West has headquarters in Calgary and has traditionally functioned as a builder of single-family houses in Calgary and Edmonton. However, it has recently expanded into Vancouver and Kamloops. The company owns 2000 acres of raw and serviced land in Alberta and British Columbia. Through partially owned joint ventures, it has access to an additional 6000 acres. These affiliated companies include Carma Developers Ltd. (owners of 3000 acres in Calgary), Base Holdings Ltd. and Sun-Del Builders Development Ltd. (Edmonton). Thus, with its affiliates, Nu-West will control over one-half of the land needs of the greater Calgary area over the next decade.

Nu-West has only recently become a rental landlord. It owns 537 units (December 31, 1971) and manages an additional 730. A company such as Nu-West is forced into the rental business by the taxation system. Naturally, a large builder is interested in acquiring control of large amounts of land. He receives the speculative gains himself, rather than paying them to somebody else. The more control one has, the less one has to compete. Unfortunately, expansion can be difficult, for one first has to acquire capital. Capital would be easier to obtain if there were no taxes, and the best way for a land developer to avoid taxes is to own rental properties on which excess depreciation can be earned, thus deferring taxes. From 1966 to 1971, Nu-West had net earnings of $10,021,523. It paid $2,303,108, representing a tax rate of 23 per cent. However, there has been a decline in its taxes paid. In 1966 Nu-West's taxes were over 30 per cent of net earnings; in 1971, its tax rate was only 14.3 per cent of net earnings. As Nu-West gets bigger and its earnings increase, it pays tax at ever diminishing rates. Nu-West improved its position to the point where, while it had 3.5 times as much in net earnings flowing into the company coffers, its contribution to the federal treasury was increased by only .05. The implementation of the tax system devised by successive governments is weighted in favour of the larger corporations, for the larger the corporation, the smaller the percentage of its book profits that are taxed.

Other benefits provided by the corporate welfare state

The above statistics must have indicated to the federal government that the impoverished corporate land developers could not survive on tax concessions alone. There can be no other explanation for government housing policies that assure the growth and oligopolistic tendencies of the corporate land developers in other ways. Certainly the intentional avoidance by government of involvement in land banking and land assembly, not to say its continuation of the present system of grants (mortgages) to land developers for limited-dividend housing, is not conducive to improving the lot of the ordinary citizens. Once again we are faced with the question, for whose benefit do governments govern?

Land banking

The Dennis report clearly details the government's avoidance of involvement in land assembly and land banking. Mr. Dennis recommended that the government engage in a major way in land banking. The object of this intrusion — and land developers need to be intruded upon — would be to control the price of land in order to reduce speculative gain. This would amount, indirectly, to controlling housing prices, and would be a far better alternative than increasing the size of mortgages, which the government insures under the NHA. The Task Force on Housing and Urban Development had recommended likewise in its report to the Trudeau government in January 1969:

> Therefore, in summary, the Task Force recommends that: The federal government should make direct loans to municipalities or regional governments to assist them in assembling and servicing land for urban growth.*

*Canada, Task Force on Housing and Urban Development, *Report* (Ottawa, 1969), p. 43.

The task force noted:

> On the basis of all the evidence and impressions before
> it, the Task Force believes that municipal assembly and
> servicing of land would produce major reductions in
> land costs in both the short and long term while encour-
> aging and assisting effective urban planning.*

A fine sentiment, but the timing was wrong. In the 1968
election campaign a Liberal brochure promised Canadians,
"We must, and we will, give top priority to meet the housing
shortage and the galloping cost of real-estate." However, by
the time the task force had made the above recommendations,
the election was long over. Asked Pierre Elliott Trudeau of the
recommendations of the Task Force on Housing and Urban
Development, "What kind of priority do you think this ought to
have? Nineteenth?**

The task force was the Liberal government's tool to create
the illusion of participatory democracy. Accordingly, the task
force travelled to every major city in Canada, listened to over
four hundred briefs and raised countless expectations, all to
no avail. For the past quarter-century no one has participated
in housing decisions except land developers and financial institutions. CMHC policies and programs are relevant only to the
needs of the corporate citizens; they are not relevant to the
ultimate client, the consumer. Given a choice between controlling prices and meeting the needs of the ordinary Canadian
taxpayer, and giving ever increasing benefits and support to
the corporate land developers, the government invariably
chooses to support the latter.

The government has the authority, under legislation already
enacted by Parliament, to engage in land assembly and land
banking, but it chooses not to do so. In 1971 the federal
government made commitments of slightly over $20 million for
land assembly.*** The figure had been $8 million in 1968 when
the present government was given its mandate, but even with
the increase the amount of money involved is not nearly suffi-

---

*p. 41.

**Reported in *Saturday Night*, October 1970.

***Canada, Central Mortgage and Housing Corporation, *Canadian
Housing Statistics* (Ottawa, 1971), p. 51.

cient. This amount is only enough to buy one-third of the land needed for public housing. It does not approach the amount needed for controlling the price of land. Moreover, in 1971 the federal government sold more residential land than it bought. The net reduction in its holdings was nearly 2000 acres.*

Low-income housing

Inertia is not the only way in which the government directly aids land developers in increasing their oligopolistic control of the land surrounding Canadian cities, control which permits them to affect the direction and rate of city development. When the government builds housing for low-income Canadians—that is, when it or the provinces build low-income housing or when limited-dividend or non-profit housing is built — it usually builds on land owned by one of the big land developers. It has no choice; they own most of it. Mr. Dennis's report details the effect of this on the consumer. For social housing the developers sell only their least accessible land and their worst land, either unserviced or located near such nuisances as expressways or railroad tracks.

> In Canada, however, virtually 80 per cent of the housing provided by the 1970 Special $200-Million Program for low-income families is dependent on the automobile for transportation. The cost of building low-density housing on marginal urban land is passed on by the developer-builder to the low-income consumer who has to underwrite the cost of transportation himself, which he can ill afford in the first place.**

This applies to both public housing and limited-dividend housing.

However, this is not the worst of it. The ordinary Canadian taxpayer pays for much of this land twice because the land developer charges him twice. When the developer files his income-tax return with the federal government, he deducts the costs of holding the land from his income. Then he turns

---

*CMHC, *Canadian Housing Statistics*, p. 51.

**Melvin Charney, *The Adequacy and Production of Low-Income Housing*, draft report for CMHC (Ottawa, 1971), p. 81.

around and includes these costs in the price of his land. He charges the government twice for these carrying costs, once when he files his income-tax return and again when he builds social housing on his inflated land. This is what the corporate welfare state is all about: Charging twice for the same commodity.

Successive federal governments have been giving handouts to the large land developers for years. It is their policies which have resulted in the appearance of these practices. But the Trudeau government has done more than other governments. Its Task Force on Housing and Urban Development recommended that:

> As a further alternative to public housing, serious consideration should be given to a program of income supplements to permit low-income families to rent or even purchase housing according to their own needs in the private market.*

The Dennis report has recommended likewise. One presumes that the recommendation of the task force represents the popular will, since it toured the country and listened to so many briefs. Implementation of this recommendation would allow the ordinary Canadian to participate in the spending of his own money. It would allow him to choose what kind of house he wanted to live in. It would allow the ordinary citizen to determine what lands would be put to use and when.

Potentially this might reduce the degree of control vested in the land developers. Not surprisingly, the recommendation was not followed. Rather, an amendment to the National Housing Act was introduced to abolish some of the limitations on the limited-dividend section which had prevented full participation by land developers. Land developers would no longer have to establish a separate corporation to build a limited-dividend housing project. Their profits would no longer be limited. They would have to agree to rent-control restrictions for only fifteen years. After that period, the housing could be withdrawn from the social-housing sector.

The previous government had let this section of the act fall into disuse. They realized that the housing produced under

---

*Canada, Task Force on Housing and Urban Development, *Report* (Ottawa, 1969), p. 57.

this government program had generally been of poor quality. Loans to corporate entrepreneurs under this program were nearly $23 million in 1968. Following the amendment to the National Housing Act in June 1969, the demands on it grew to nearly $90 million for the remainder of 1969. Then the Trudeau government cut back the expansion of the money supply and raised interest rates to the exorbitant levels at which they largely remain now. The result was that land developers could not get loan funds, and it appeared in late 1969 that a repeat of the decline in housing starts experienced in 1966 would take place. The government could have chosen to react to the situation by building more public housing to provide some relief for those who cannot afford to pay the rents charged by land developers; predictably, it chose to meet the situation by channelling more funds to the corporate land developers. Loans to land developers in 1970 for housing built under the limited-dividend program and for assisted home-ownership — another government program which the ordinary Canadian taxpayer can use only by consuming shelter provided by the "free"-enterprising developers — amounted to $372,205,000; $240 million of this was for the Special Innovative Program. Perhaps the Trudeau government thought that it could not do such a favour for the real-estate industry without the Canadian taxpayer feeling a bit uneasy, so it rationalized the give-away program designed to elicit housing innovations.

The Charney report provides evidence on just how much innovation occurred and illustrates the fact that innovation was only a rationale for enlarging programs which use land developers as conduits for providing housing for Canadians. Charney concludes:

> Housing built during the past fifteen years tends towards higher densities, a limited range of standardized accommodation, reduced variety, limited common facilities and a segregation of unit types. What is presently being built is largely the same kind of housing as produced during the last fifteen years.*

Mr. Charney quotes from a CMHC memo of March 3, 1970, which sets out what was meant by innovation:

> . . . elements which must be given consideration include

---

*Charney, *Low-Income Housing*, p. 84.

standard relaxations, reduced lot sizes, increased density.*

Moreover, the Dennis report emphasizes that the housing built is hardly adequate for families. The proportion of apartment units in housing increased from 33 to 77 per cent in the two years from 1968 to 1970. The proportion in high-rise apartments has increased from 12 to 45 per cent in these two years. In 1970, 84 per cent of the housing units built in metropolitan Toronto were in high-rise apartments. It was 100 per cent in Halifax and Edmonton. The number of bedrooms included in the units is declining as well. In 1968, 63.1 per cent had three or more bedrooms. In 1970, only 40.9 per cent had three or more bedrooms. In addition, Mr. Dennis concludes that:

> The degree of under-utilization of units is shocking. Twenty-six per cent of the families in three or more bedroom units had a spare bedroom. It is obvious that the units were not created with the needs of the consumer in mind. These figures would also indicate a "creaming" process in choosing the type of tenant acceptable, particularly in areas where developers have a lock on the market and where occupancy rates are high.**

These are the evaluations which others have made of the dwellings that the "free"-enterprising developers built under the Special Innovative Program. What most Canadians do not realize is that the housing built under this program is also an integral part of the corporate welfare state. The owners of these dwellings get to deduct capital-cost allowances for tax purposes. Of course, they do not pass this saving on to the low-income tenant.

In the next decade land developers will be allowed capital-cost deductions to the extent of an estimated $150 million. $470 millions have been given to land developers in the three years 1969–1971, while in the next decade land developers will be allowed capital-cost deductions to the extent of an estimated $150 million. Their actual depreciation will probably be only $75 million. They will, therefore, receive interest-free loans

*p. 87.
**p. 428.

in the amount of $75 million. It is also entirely possible that this manifestation of free enterprise would be just that to the developer — free, since he could go into a project without investing one cent of his own capital.

A prime example was described in the Charney report to the CMHC Task Force on Low-Income Housing. According to the report, Victoria Wood Development Corporation received a commitment from CMHC for a $14-million loan in July 1970 for the construction of Main Square, a high-rise development containing 1800 units. Half of the units were to be rented at subsidized rates, and the other half at market rates. CMHC and Victoria Wood were to share the surplus from commercial rents and subsidize the low-rent units accordingly. The company was also given a $40,000 advertising budget to help remove the "stigma" of the development and to make rent subsidies known to prospective tenants.

Nevertheless, the advertising campaign for Main Square omitted mention of the subsidies, so that low-income people were not aware they were available. Less than 25 per cent of this low-income housing is being used by low-income tenants, according to the Charney report. Rents on three-quarters of the units are far above low-income scale. Victoria Wood, meanwhile, collects a fat fee for managing the development.

The public, through CMHC, put up the money; the company collects the profits, and very few low-income people benefit from the project.

Taxes and planned premature obsolescence

Many Canadians are upset by the rapid rate at which larger housing units in their inner cities have been allowed to deteriorate and to be razed for parking lots or commercial buildings. The inner city has traditionally been the most reliable source of housing for large families with limited means. Roomy housing at reasonable rents is not being built. It is certainly not being built under the public-housing program.

The disappearance of inner-city housing has reached crisis proportions. It has evoked outcries from citizens' organizations in every major urban centre in Canada. However, the corporations can't see why people would be upset at the loss of their homes and the lack of housing at reasonable prices. An example is a statement made by A. E. Diamond, president of Cadillac Development Corporation Ltd., in his 1971 annual report:

> The objections now being raised by the pressure groups to some applications for re-zoning to denser forms of accommodation are short-sighted and, indeed, irrational because they undoubtedly will result in fewer housing starts in the built-up areas of our cities . . .

Of course, his idea of a housing start is replacing five-bedroom homes with a one- or two-bedroom high-rise apartment. It is also part of the CMHC syndrome for developers to measure their success in the number of starts they generate, regardless of what these starts do to existing housing stock or whether the starts have any real relation to consumer needs. The Dennis report recommended that:

> The federal government should (as it did with urban renewal) freeze all further funding under the NHA of private centre-city redevelopment in excess of 15 units, while it reviews the costs and benefits of that process.*

Of course, no word has been heard on this proposal yet. Nor will it be, for the federal government and urban land developers use the taxation system as a vehicle to eliminate large low-rental housing units in the inner city. Local municipalities are probably only too happy to aid in this elimination because old houses do not produce enough tax revenue to pay for the larger roads and sewers needed to service the high-rise office structures downtown. It should be stressed that local councils are not the prime actor in this event; they only play a strong supporting role. The prime actors are the land developers and the federal government.

It is incredible in this day and age that the average Canadian citizen, who is better educated, knows more, and understands more, is afforded so little opportunity to influence the decisions that affect his life and his country's future.

The federal government can do two things to slow the process of inner-city decay. It can hand over tax monies to the municipalities so that municipal officials can conduct proper town planning, independent of the corporate land developers.

---

*p. 17.

Secondly, the federal government should modify the taxation system so that there are fewer benefits for the developers tearing down existing housing stock. Present tax legislation is biased in favour of the demolition of existing housing. We have seen that no "free"-enterprising corporate developer can pass up an opportunity to increase his cash flow.

The regulations for capital-cost allowances increase the chances of a home being demolished when it changes owners. While a developer has owned a house or apartment building as a landlord, he has enjoyed the advantages of deferred taxes from the excessive capital-cost allowances offered by successive federal governments. This is an interest-free loan. If he sells the house and gets more for it than he's told the government it's worth, he has to pay back to the government part of the loan, since he recovered some of the excess depreciation claimed. But if he convinces the purchaser that it's in his interest to demolish it, or demolishes it himself, then the building is written off completely, even if it had a few more years of depreciable life left. Having done so, the owner doesn't have to repay his loan. He gets a windfall gain. That's how the taxation system works.

In addition to encouraging premature demolition of large inner-city houses, the taxation system encourages inadequate maintenance. It does this in two ways. First, it encourages rapid turnover in the property. As soon as a landlord has depreciated most of the value of his property, it is only natural for him to sell it. The new owner can then take advantage of accelerated capital-cost write-offs himself; the old owner can buy another house or building and get the benefits of accelerated capital-cost allowances.

We know that buildings are less adequately maintained if they change owners frequently. Each owner is encouraged to try and pass on maintenance costs to the next owner. The result is that nobody cares for the building. Often, the landlord has the effrontery to suggest that it's careless tenants who cause inadequate maintenance.

There is a second way in which inadequate maintenance is encouraged. This is especially so if the landlord has a small operation. If the landlord is a large corporation, he gets interest-free loans from excess capital-cost allowances. But if he's a small individual taxpayer who just happens to own a house or two — maybe he's a pensioner and he depends on income from the houses to support him — he doesn't get nearly as large a loan because he can't write off excess depreciation allowances against non-rental income. For him the loophole was closed in 1971.

If he's wealthy he can afford to maintain the building. If he's not, and the building is old and large items need replacement, he may have difficulty making the necessary repairs and replacements. Taxation regulations will consider many of these items to be capital investments; consequently, they cannot be written off in a single year as can maintenance costs. Many maintenance items become necessary because of inadequate maintenance in the past. In this way the small landlord is discriminated against by the taxation system.

The taxation system also discriminates against the average Canadian who needs shelter for his family. The system works against comprehensive planning, confuses priorities, misallocates funds, discriminates against maintenance and operation of existing housing stock, induces wide-spread destruction of such stock for high-density rental dwellings and effectively puts a large portion of the Canadian population at the mercy of the whims and vagaries of the corporate developer landlords. Government has recreated the feudal lords. These modern barons control most of the land available for housing around our major cities, while the inner cities have become the personal fiefdom of the corporate landlords.

CHAPTER FIVE

Solutions of the Past

> We must strike at the root of economic disparity,
> putting behind us the easy subsidized solutions
> of the past.
> —*from The Just Society, 1968 Election Campaign*

For years Canadians have been talking about regional disparity
and the hardship endured by those who live in the poorer areas
of this country. Consequently, the Regional Development Incentives Act (RDIA) give-away plan is one of particular interest
to Canadians.

When Pierre Trudeau presented himself to the Canadian
voters in 1968, he refused to make many specific promises.
But he did make two: to alleviate poverty in those parts of
Canada which had suffered most, and to reform our biased
election practices which permit some political parties to rely
on the financial contributions of big businesses and rich
individuals.

Mr. Trudeau assured Canadian voters that his election-
reform pledge would be assigned "top priority," but for four
years nothing was done. Finally, in an attempt to ward off
increasing criticism by the press and the public on its failure
to act on this specific promise, the government introduced a
watered-down bill in the dying days of Parliament which failed
to deal in any significant way with election contributions, and
which the government knew full well could not be passed
before Parliament adjourned.

In contrast, the promise to alleviate regional disparities received immediate attention from the government. A new min-
istry was created—the Department of Regional Economic
Expansion, better known as DREE. The new department was
given a tool in the Regional Development Incentives Act, under
which public funds would be distributed to corporations willing
to locate new plants in certain "designated" areas.

Since the beginning of this "incentives" program in July
1969, DREE has allocated a total of $265 million which has

gone, with few exceptions, to private corporations.

The prompt generosity shown to private enterprise and delays in implementing the election expenses promise must have pleased both the corporations and the party campaign fund raisers. But what has been done for the people of Canada, particularly those living in the regions which had most to expect from Mr. Trudeau's promises?

Leaving aside the interesting question of the effectiveness of grants to private industry as a main regional-development tool, let us examine the geographic distribution of RDIA grants. The following table demonstrates what actually happened.

The Dollar Value of RDIA Grants[1]
(percentage distribution)

	Atlantic %	Quebec %	Ontario %	West %	Canada %
July 1969–June 1971	28.6	36.8	10.5	24.3	100.0
3rd quarter of 1971	33.5	42.0	6.8	18.0	100.0
4th quarter of 1971	18.1	61.5	8.5	11.9	100.0
1st quarter of 1972	12.8	74.8	5.8	6.8	100.0

SOURCE: DREE reports to Parliament.

1. Offers made by DREE and accepted by recipients.

It appears that the share of grants received by the various regions in the first two years were not altogether out of line with the social and economic needs of those regions. However, in the summer of 1971 the pattern started to change. By March 1972, it had been completely altered. The Atlantic provinces' share of the money dropped to 12.8 per cent, Ontario's share to 5.8 per cent and the western provinces' share to 6.8 per cent. The big gainer was Quebec, whose share had risen from 36.8 per cent to 75 per cent of the total.

I am fully conscious of the urgent needs in Quebec and do not begrudge the people of that province any assistance they receive. But the timing interests and disturbs me. The distribution pattern changed as the election drew nearer. Was Mr. Marchand acting in his capacity as minister or as leader for his party in Quebec?

Mr. Marchand is, of course, quite unaware of what's happening in his department. By his own admission he sees only a very few applications while his bureaucrats handle the rest of them. This is a very prudent arrangement for a minister who doubles as the co-chairman of the Liberal campaign.

It would be indeed unwise, not to say indecent, for Mr. Marchand to hand out public funds to private corporations with his right hand, while at the same time collecting campaign funds for the Liberal Party with his left hand. Mr. Marchand, however, is careful to ensure that his right hand does not know what his left hand is doing. As he solemnly declared in the House of Commons on March 2, 1972: "I have never collected a cent for the Liberal party; as leader for Quebec, and responsible for Quebec, I merely sent a letter of invitation to a fund-raising cocktail." It was an innocent letter: it stated that "funds must be available so that work of the party, in the next few months, may be adequately financed."

Two reliable authorities have indicated the extent to which the Conservatives and Liberals are allied with big business.

According to K. Z. Paltiel, director of research for the Barbeau Committee on Election Expenses: "The most obvious generalization to be made about the finances of Canada's two older parties is that they look almost exclusively to business for the supply of their campaign funds. Both the Liberals and Conservatives have tried with varying degrees of enthusiasm to widen the base of financial support. To date these efforts have been a failure."*

"Material gain, policy decisions, the choice of leaders, and the general course of government activity have all been counters in the effort to provide funds for the parties. At the lowest level, the price has been concessions, dispensations and specific acts of patronage; at a higher level the aim has been to 'stabilize the field for corporate activity.' In both cases contributions have assured access to the decision-making authorities in party and government."**

The implications of Professor Paltiel's statement were emphasized by Liberal Party fund raiser R. G. Renkin, who told a Liberal convention in Ottawa on February 14, 1972:

*K. Z. Paltiel, *Political Party Financing in Canada* (Toronto: McGraw-Hill, 1970), p. 42.

**p. 161.

"The Liberal Party has operated for many years on the support of ninety-five major Canadian corporations."

However, we digress from the main topic, which is the corporate welfare system.

In the case of DREE, the system has a few more angles yet. As Mr. Marchand said, he deals with only a few applications for grants. Who then makes the decisions on the others?

Mr. Marchand has a so-called Industrial Incentives Advisory Board, which meets monthly to discuss the grants.

Who are the members? Apart from a few federal bureaucrats, the board is composed of one labour representative and four business representatives: Mr. J. B. Estey, executive vice-president of National Sea Products Ltd.; Mr. E. Kendall Cork, vice-president and treasurer of Noranda Mines Ltd.; Mr. M. W. MacKenzie, chairman of the board (retired), Chemcell Ltd.; and Mr. Robert H. Jones, executive vice-president and chief executive officer, Investors Group (Winnipeg).

National Sea Products, Mr. Estey's firm, is a thriving corporation in the Atlantic provinces. It is one of the four largest fish companies in North America in sales, but it was not that prosperous a few years ago. Federal grants have helped.

Before the RDIA legislation of 1969, the company was offered altogether $1,280,953 in grants for regional-development purposes. Between May 1970 and September 1971, under RDIA, it was offered by Mr. Marchand's department a total of $2,408,378 for its four plants located in Nova Scotia, Newfoundland and Prince Edward Island. In addition, in 1968–69 it received $25,439 from the Department of Industry, Trade and Commerce under the PAIT program. Finally, the company had some fish trawlers built at the Dosco shipyard, which received from the federal government $6,064,796 between 1965 and 1969.

The latter grant was actually given to Dosco and not to National Sea Products, as Mr. W. O. Morrow, the president of the company, was quick to point out when this fact was first revealed last August. According to him, without the federal shipbuilding subsidy the company would have been forced to buy cheaper vessels abroad. Not so. The chairman of the board of the company, Mr. H. D. O'Connor, stated on July 23, 1970, at the hearings of the Parliamentary Standing Committee on Finance, Trade and Commerce, that the company was able "over the past six years" to invest $22 million in vessels, plant and equipment. "A substantial part of the cash required to make this investment came from the cash flow which resulted from claiming capital-cost allowances at regular rates and at the accelerated rates permitted by incentive legislation. That is, 33⅓ per cent on trawlers, 20 per cent on buildings and 50 per cent on equipment ... claiming capital-cost allowances a rapidly expanding company such as National can defer payment of much or all of the taxes otherwise payable until a later year."

The government has so far offered the company over $9 million. Some of this money has already been spent; the rest of it is ready to be collected.

Meanwhile, the company has returned to the public $1.5 million in income tax in the last seven years, a rate of 5.2 per cent on net earnings. Net profits in those same years amounted to $8 million, not including rapidly increasing assets.

Noranda Mines is one of the exceptionally prosperous mining corporations operating in Canada. As the annual report proudly says, Noranda is: "a billion-dollar corporation: 92 per cent owned by 31,000 Canadians." Net profits for the last seven years came up to $351 million. How much income tax Noranda actually paid only the tax collector and Mr. Cork know.

In March 1971 the company was offered a DREE grant of $3,522,000, which it gratefully accepted. In the years between 1968–70 it solicited and received $956,610 from the Department of Industry, Trade and Commerce under the PAIT program.

Noranda owns 99 per cent of another mining company, Gaspé Copper Mines, also a prosperous enterprise. Between 1965 and 1971 Gaspé made a net profit of $66 million. It paid some income tax, but again how much is unknown. Relying on Mr. Marchand's statutory monthly reports to Parliament, it was estimated that Gaspé Copper was offered a $1,155,500 grant from DREE. So it was. What was not known was that the reports were incomplete. Last April Mr. Marchand inadvertently revealed that some RDIA grants had been increased without the knowledge of Parliament. The grant to Gaspé Copper was one of these. The vice-president and treasurer of Noranda was appointed to Mr. Marchand's advisory committee on grants in May 1971. Shortly after, in November to be exact, this Noranda subsidiary accepted an additional grant of $2,111,-500.

Chemcell Ltd., now known as Celanese Canada Ltd., is a subsidiary of a giant, US-owned textile and chemical company. Its dealings with the Liberal government are of considerable interest.

Between January and March of 1970 it accepted four grants from DREE for its three plants in Quebec which totalled $568,143. Shortly thereafter the company decided to consolidate its weaving operations within two plants, so shutting down the Montmagny plant. This decision required that Chemcell decline the grant of $70,245 for that plant. The result: 450 laid-off workers.

When the Montmagny layoffs came up in Parliament, Mr. Marchand went to Celanese for help. Mr. Jim Hynes, Celanese manager of corporate affairs, told the *Toronto Star* (August 17, 1972): "Marchand seemed to be quite concerned about this. He even came to us to ask us to provide him with information on new jobs so he could defend the grants in Parliament. We weren't able to do that because there weren't any new jobs. We told him to take the tack that without the grant perhaps some old jobs would have been lost. He wasn't very impressed."

The abandoned Montmagny plant was purchased by Consolidated Textiles Mills Ltd. and Dionne Spinning Ltd. These two companies evolved a good scheme for creating jobs—436 to be precise. For that favour Mr. Marchand offered them a total of $2,477,600 in grants. This deal was closed between November 1971 and February 1972.

In sum, Mr. Marchand reported to Parliament that he had created fifteen jobs in the Celanese plants and 436 jobs in the revived Montmagny plant—at a total cost to the taxpayer of $2,975,498. What he had chosen to ignore was that in the shuffle, 450 workers lost their jobs.

The record is now clear. Mr. Marchand has found 451 new jobs, has lost 450 old jobs, and in the process has spent nearly $3 million.

It is not known what price Celanese got for its abandoned textile mill. The successor companies accepted DREE money in the winter of 1971–72. A few months earlier, Mr. MacKenzie, former chairman of Celanese, had become advisor to Mr.

Marchand.

The companies involved are not what anyone would call "good corporate citizens." In 1971 Celanese Canada paid $248,-000 in income tax on net earnings of $9.7 million, a rate of 2.6 per cent. Between 1967 and 1971 Consolidated Textile Mills paid a total of $3555 income tax on net earnings of $5.7 million and net profits of $1.8 million. Corresponding data for the third company involved are not available.

The Investors Group has close ties with at least 160 corporations, among them Canadian Pacific, Power Corporation, Imperial Life Assurance and Bramalea Consolidated Developments. There is no record of DREE grants given to the Investors Group. Mr. Jones, with his vast business experience and his vast corporate connections, is ideally placed to advise the minister on incentive grants in their present context.

Last spring NDP members of Parliament called Mr. Marchand's attention to the potential conflict of interest arising from the appointment of so many prominent businessmen to a board which advises the minister on grants to industry. The minister shrugged the warning off: "The only thing we can do, and this is what we are doing, is ask anyone who has an interest in the case to reveal his interest so that people know damn well that Mr. X, who is at the table and is trying to support such a case, is a vice-president of the company. Well, I gave you the names [of the members of the Advisory Board] and I think that most of them are interested, not in any particular industry but in public interest . . ."

No sooner had Mr. Marchand disposed of this matter to his own satisfaction, than another fuse blew in the DREE grant system. It was the McCain case.

The McCain family of New Brunswick makes its fortune on the potatoes grown on its own 10,000 acres (Valley Farm Ltd.). It sells fertilizer (McCain Fertilizer Ltd.) and farm machinery (Thomas Equipment Ltd.) to other growers; it buys and processes potatoes, vegetables and other fruit (McCain Foods Ltd.) and stores them (Carleton Cold Storage Co. Ltd.). It transports its products (Day & Ross Ltd.) in a fleet of more than six hundred trucks and trailers, selling them all over the world.

The keystone to this growing fortune is the new $7-million potato-processing plant at Florenceville, New Brunswick.

At some point between 1965 and 1969 the company negotiated for a development grant under the RDIA's predecessor, receiving $596,221. In August 1969 the company had the honour of being offered the first grant under the new Regional Development Incentives Act—a grant of $2,925,000. In accordance with the law, that amount was reported to Parliament. On April 27, 1972, the minister inadvertently revealed to the Standing Committee on Regional Development that McCain had been offered $6.1 million. Under questioning Mr. Marchand had to admit this. At a later date DREE offered McCain another grant of $633,000 and later another one of $443,900. In sum, McCain could count on $7,772,221 from the federal government.

To simplify matters, the chronology of the dealings is outlined below:

	Date of application	Date of offer	Date offer accepted
1. grant of $6.1 million	Dec. 19/69	Nov. 2/70	Dec. 9/70
2. grant of $633,000	May 22/70	Aug. 28/70	Sept. 14/70
3. grant of $443,000	June 8/70	July 22/70	Aug. 3/70

A certain Mr. G. McClure joined DREE on February 24, 1969. He left the department seventeen months later, on August 1, 1970. In the department he held the position of Director of Operations for the East (Atlantic). After having left DREE, he joined the firm of McCain Foods Ltd. in a senior capacity.

On May 10, 1972, Mr. Marchand and his deputy minister revealed in the House of Commons that their review of relevant files "failed to reveal any evidence that would give rise to legitimate concern about a conflict of interests . . .Mr. McClure . . . was called in for consultations and discussions on the subject [of grants to McCain]. But the responsibility for the evaluation of the applications was clearly carried by officers of the Incentives Division and the then Deputy Minister."

On September 9, 1972, a story in a Toronto newspaper revealed that two officers of DREE had been suspended without pay a few weeks previously in connection with a grant of $736,970 to Silver Shields Mines. According to the minister the suspension related to the officials' purchase of the stock "at a moment when it was not felt to be proper."

One could continue analyzing individual grants, but the list of contentious cases is too long. For example: Michelin ($14,-899,380); Digital Components ($1,511,000); Union Carbide ($1,998,900); Rayonnier Quebec-ITT ($13,770,000); B.F. Goodrich ($1,165,700); Glaverbel Verrerie ($3,845,700); Falconbridge ($4,000,240); Micro-Max Products ($1,392,585); Ecstall Mining ($7,819,000); Procter & Gamble ($15,793,125); IBM ($6,003,750).

And the multimillion-dollar give-aways have continued into the current election campaign. In a last-minute attempt to placate Gaspé residents, who for years now have been getting the short end of the stick, Mr. Marchand announced on September 20, 1972, in grandstand fashion a grant of $5.3 million for a liner-board mill in Cabano, with a promise of considering an additional subsidy of $4.7 million.*

Individual grants aside, is the theory behind the grant-to-private-corporations concept sound? DREE has set out to alleviate—if not to remove—the very same regional disparities which are the result, in large part, of the workings of unbridled free enterprise. By giving handouts to corporate giants DREE hopes to change their ways. What a vain hope!

The grant give-away started modestly enough. In the first year, 1966–67, only $1.2 million was doled out. But the groundwork had been laid for bigger things. The following year expenditures rose to $15.4 million; by 1971–72 the government was doling out $116 million. Last spring the minister asked Parliament to give him authority to hand out $174 million in the current fiscal year. All together this adds up to $437 million in so-called incentive grants.

Mr. Marchand has been releasing data almost daily on just how many jobs his grants would create; the latest figure approaches 60,000. Somehow it has not been reflected in the unemployment figures, nor in other statistics which measure economic disparities.

Last spring a Dr. Springate from the Harvard School of Business volunteered to testify before the House of Commons Committee on Regional Development.

Dr. Springate, after an exhaustive investigation of a sampling of DREE grant recipients, found that the effect of the grant program on investment decision was small: "Movement of location of plants within Canada is minimal, and significantly, grants

*See the *New Liskeard* story of June 1968 in chapter six.

produce few changes in respect to project timing, project size or technology used." Dr. Springate pronounced the fateful verdict: "Roughly half of the incentive grants do not influence investment in any significant manner, and can be considered to be windfall gains."

Mr. Marchand and other Liberals on the committee were upset; they dismissed Dr. Springate as being "naïve," but were unable to point to any other analysis which arrived at different conclusions.

Three months later a secret Treasury Board memorandum delivered the coup de grâce. It confirmed that some businesses aren't telling DREE the whole truth about their needs when they apply for the grants and that it is therefore "imperative" that a serious examination of DREE be launched. The memorandum confirmed that Dr. Springate's report contained "evidence which verifies some of the worst fears of observers of the RDIA program."

Thus ends four years of the Trudeau–Marchand "fight" against regional disparities. Many corporations have benefitted from DREE windfalls; some have grown rich. There were even jobs created in some cases. But when the results are measured against the public resources dissipated, the RDIA program is not something the government can boast of.

Regional economic development is one of Canada's most urgent tasks, and without assistance from the public treasury it cannot be fulfilled; it cannot even be begun. But the program must be planned; the grants must serve their job-creating purpose. They cannot be permitted to become an election pork-barrel, or to be used to hand out windfall gains to corporations.

We should have more, not less, assistance to the disadvantaged areas of Canada. The present program must be fundamentally changed.

CHAPTER SIX

Alphabet Soup

DREE is not the only government department heavily involved in the corporate welfare rip-off. Jean Luc Pépin's Department of Industry, Trade and Commerce is also a contributor. In fact, this department administers twelve give-away programs that we know of. The list of their names reads like a veritable alphabet soup: AAA, BEAM, DIP, ESP, GAAP, IDAP, IRDIA, MACH, PAIT, PEP, PIDA, SCSP.

SCSP

One of Mr. Pépin's principal contributions to corporate welfare is the relatively unknown Ship Construction Subsidy Program (SCSP).

Ottawa has been subsidizing the shipbuilding industry since the late 1940s, always on an on-again, off-again basis, never with a carefully thought-out, long-range plan in mind. Since the revamping of the program by the Conservative government in 1961, the industry has been receiving about $30 million annually from the federal coffers.

Currently, SCSP subsidies cover 18½ per cent of the cost of commercial vessels built in Canadian yards for Canadian customers. Steel fishing trawlers receive a 35 per cent subsidy. Commercial vessels built for foreign firms are subsidized at 13 to 16 per cent, depending on their size, though this is a special program slated to end in 1975.

The amount of money involved has been substantial: $309 million between 1961 and 1971. In the last six years more than half the total of all shipbuilding grants has gone to four corporations: Saint John Shipbuilding and Dry Dock Co. Ltd., Port Weller Dry Dock Ltd., Canada Steamship Lines and Hawker-Siddeley.

Unfortunately such largesse has not resulted in many new jobs for our growing labour force. According to Statistics Canada, the shipbuilding and repair industry employed only 14,900 persons at the end of 1971, an increase of less than

1500 (or 3.1 per cent) during a period in which Ottawa pumped almost $300 million of public funds into the shipyards. In other words, that federal subsidy amounted to about $20,000 per job in the past ten years. It is astounding that the cost of one new job was equivalent to something like one-third of the total wage bill for the industry.

However, the government does not claim that the purpose of the program is to create jobs. Government statements emphasize that the objective is to develop "a healthy and viable shipbuilding industry." After more than twenty years and hundreds of millions of dollars, this goal is as distant as ever. What then has been achieved?

In the case of Canada Steamship Lines (CSL), the achievement appears to be clear. A CSL wholly owned subsidiary, Davie Shipbuilding Ltd. of Lauzon, Quebec, received $24.3 million in ship-construction grants in the 1965–1970 period. At the same time, another CSL wholly owned subsidiary, Canadian Shipbuilding and Engineering Ltd. of Collingwood and Thunder Bay, Ontario, received $16.7 million. The CSL complex received a total of $41 million. Meanwhile, the parent company showed net earnings over the period of $145.6 million, and profits of $48.1 million. Without a single penny of public money, this company could have employed its shipbuilding work force throughout the period, could have maintained the same wages and could *still* have reaped profits of more than $7 million.

In these same years, the CSL complex returned to the government $23.6 million in income tax. Net loss to the taxpayer in this deal was $17.4 million.

That is not all. Some of the vessels constructed by Davie and Canadian Shipbuilding and Engineering during that period were built for their parent corporation. A convenient provision in the income-tax rules allows rapid write-offs of Canadian-built ships, which gives CSL the right to depreciate the entire capital cost of these ships in three years, rather than the normal seven-year period.

The shipbuilders benefit. The shipowners benefit. But does the public benefit?

Take another example. During 1965–1970, Ottawa ladled out more than $13 million in ship-construction subsidies to St. John Shipbuilding and Dry Dock Co. Ltd. (Its president is J. K.

Irving, the son of K. C. Irving.) DREE also kicked in $1.8 million to assist in the expansion of shipyard facilities. Not much information on the financial affairs of Saint John Shipbuilding during the period is available. Only in the past year have privately held companies been required to file skeleton financial statements with the federal government for public inspection. But we do know something about the Irving empire as a whole. A conservative estimate of its assets is that they are well over half a billion dollars. That fortune was amassed in only forty years, a good part of it during the Second World War. Probably such a rapid accumulation could not have been achieved without the assistance of our tax system.

Not satisfied with the $15 million in federal grants, J. K. Irving has his eyes on a potential new source of government generosity. Speaking at the christening of his vessels constructed with the help of corporate welfare, J. K. turned to his guest of honour, DREE Minister Jean Marchand, and suggested that Ottawa adopt a policy of subsidizing the *operation* of a Canadian merchant marine. The Irving Line would no doubt be an appropriate name for it.

Not all of Canada's shipbuilding industry is as profitable as Canada Steamship Lines or the Irving empire. But the federal government does not discriminate in favour of the weak. Rich or poor, efficient or otherwise, federal largesse is distributed blindly, without any plan and without any concept of how a healthy shipbuilding industry should be put together.

Take the case of the now defunct George T. Davie Ltd., which used to operate a yard in Lauzon, Quebec. This Davie is an entirely separate company from the already discussed Davie Shipbuilding Ltd. In the six years from the beginning of the revised subsidy program in 1961 until the yard's demise in 1968, George T. Davie received $9.4 million in ship-construction grants. Its parent company, Canadian Vickers Ltd., had itself received over $14 million in ship subsidies during the same period. In 1968 Vickers sold the assets of the George Davie yard to Davie Shipbuilding Ltd., which operated a yard next door on the St. Lawrence in Lauzon, and which had been the recipient of a cool $35 million in ship subsidies since 1962.

All this corporate welfare did not contribute to the well-being of the Lauzon shipworkers. Layoffs began almost immediately, and the worst fears of the employees were soon confirmed when Vickers announced that it would close the George Davie yard for good in June 1968. Such an action would have thrown a thousand men out of work.

The federal government panicked. June was an election month and, in a desperate attempt to keep the yard open until after polling day, the Navy was ordered to find a ship—"any ship"—and send it to Lauzon for repairs. The only vessel available was the *New Liskeard*, an obscure oceanographic survey ship, moored in Halifax awaiting minor repairs. The government's decision was proudly announced by Jean Marchand two weeks before election day, with the promise that more government contracts would be forthcoming. Just six weeks later, the same Mr. Marchand, safely re-elected in his Quebec City riding across the river from the *New Liskeard* at the George Davie yard, stated that the cost would be several times higher than expected, and that in the interest of economy the repairs would not be undertaken. The yard died.

But there is more to this story than a plant closure and an example of political opportunism. At the very time that it was closing its Lauzon yard, Canadian Vickers Ltd., with the generous financial support of Joey Smallwood, was opening a new, $14-million shipyard at Marystown in Newfoundland. Did Canada need another shipyard? How did the Lauzon shutdown and the new Marystown yard mesh with federal government policy towards the industry?

Mr. Marchand, then in charge of the Department of Manpower and Immigration, had found an easy way out. He offered the laid-off Quebec workers mobility grants to move with their families to the new shipyard in Newfoundland. Only two moved. It was an easy solution for Mr. Marchand, but not for the French-speaking workers.

It is obvious that if Canada wants a viable shipbuilding industry, the government must help. But public support should only be forthcoming after a thorough assessment of the prospects for a permanent industry, and with a careful consideration of the areas in which Canadian shipbuilders can specialize efficiently. If it is shown that long-term prospects for a Canadian shipbuilding industry are reasonable, then the government should make the same demand of the industry that a private investor would make; equity in return for the use of its money, including a share in management to ensure that the taxpayers' money is well spent. This is one industry in which a revamped Canada Development Corporation might well invest with effectiveness.

DIP

Most of us will remember the day of February 20, 1959, when Conservative Prime Minister John Diefenbaker pronounced the death sentence upon the Canadian-designed fighter plane CF 105, known as the Avro Arrow. Some years later, the Liberal minister of National Defence announced the end of yet another ambitious Canadian venture, the all-terrain troop carrier Bobcat. More recently we have seen the hydrofoil *Bras d'Or* placed in mothballs. Hundreds of millions of dollars of taxpayers' money were wasted on these military ventures.

Quite obviously, there is no room left for Canada's ambitions to develop and produce sophisticated military hardware. Our own needs are very limited and the military superpowers could hardly be expected to rely on us to do that job for them.

The Trudeau government realistically recognized our limited role in international military affairs. It reduced our military manpower and the capital expenditures for equipment. However, the defence industry in Canada (it cannot be called a Canadian defence industry) proved to be a much tougher customer to deal with. Federal cash grants to that industry still continue unabated.

Under the Defence Industry Productivity (DIP) program and its predecessors, the federal government has given the defence industry a gift of $214.4 million in the last six years. Moreover, the government estimates a further expenditure of $85,800,000 in the next two fiscal years.

The official pamphlet of the Department of Industry, Trade and Commerce explains the purpose of this program:

> The aim of such assistance is to strengthen the competence of such industries to participate in production-sharing opportunities that exist in the world market and to take advantage of any unique high technology which has been acquired through Canadian research and development.

Federal public accounts give the names of firms and the

amounts of grants given them from year to year. The nature of the projects is veiled by a screen of secrecy. Only historians will be able to tell us which grants resulted in technological development, in increased exports or in the creation of jobs for Canadians, and which grants ended up in the profit columns of corporations.

The pattern of these give-aways suggests that only a few sizable corporations are favoured by the federal government. Between 1965 and 1971, ten corporations alone consumed 78.8 per cent of the available money. And the famous report on foreign investment by Revenue Minister Herb Gray revealed that between 1964 and 1971, 86.2 per cent of the grant money went to foreign-controlled corporations.

Who are the principal beneficiaries of this particular government generosity? Have a close look at the following table.

Reprinted with permission of Miller Services Ltd., Toronto

"For Pete's sake—don't waste your time on the crum eaters!"

DIP Grants 1965–1966 to 1970–1971

	$ million	% of total DIP grants
1. United Aircraft of Canada Ltd. (subsidiary of United Aircraft Corp., USA)	32.7	17.0
2. Douglas Aircraft of Canada (subsidiary of McDonnell Douglas, USA)	26.3	13.6
3. Canadair Ltd. (subsidiary of General Dynamics Corp., USA)	20.7	10.7
4. Canadian Marconi (Canadian controlled)	20.6	10.7
5. The Hawker-Siddeley complex (de Havilland Aircraft of Canada Ltd.; Hawker-Siddeley Canada Ltd.; Orenda Ltd. All are subsidiaries of Hawker-Siddeley of England.)	18.9	9.8
6. The Bell Canada complex (Northern Electric; Microsystems International. Both are subsidiaries of Bell Canada. Canadian controlled)	13.2	6.9
7. CAE Industries Ltd. (Canadian controlled)	9.7	5.0
8. Computing Devices of Canada Ltd. (subsidiary of Control Data Corp., USA)	9.4	4.9
9. Bristol Aerospace Ltd. (subsidiary of Rolls Royce, UK)	2.7	1.4
10. Garrett Manufacturing Ltd. (subsidiary of Garrett Corp., USA)	2.4	1.2
Total	156.5	81.4

By far the largest grants went to the aircraft industry. That industry, as federal Minister of Transport Don Jamieson admitted last May, is in trouble. The industry is also in trouble in the United States and in western Europe. Only four years ago the industry employed 45,000 people in Canada; employment has dropped to 24,000 in 1972, and the Air Industries

Association projects a drop to 15,000 within the foreseeable future.

Practically all of Canada's aircraft-manufacturing industry is controlled from abroad. Needless to say, the world-wide slump in the industry affected the foreign-controlled branch plants in Canada before it affected their parent companies. How much more money will the federal government have to spend in order to prevent a complete collapse of these foreign-owned factories?

In 1971, the four leading aircraft firms (United Aircraft, Douglas Aircraft, Canadair, Hawker-Siddeley) showed strange performance. While receiving $17.3 million in DIP grants, they declared only $3.2 million for income taxes, most of this in the "deferred" category. The taxpayer pitched in more than $17 million, and yet the layoffs continue.

The DIP game is not restricted to the aircraft industry. Between 1967 and 1970, Canadian Marconi received $18.3 million in DIP grants while paying income taxes of $4.5 million. Canadian taxpayers lost over $13 million to a company that has a record of fluctuating employment.

Northern Electric and its subsidiaries (including Microsystems International) are being financed from the federal kitty at a reckless rate. Between 1965 and 1970, they pocketed $13.2 million in DIP grants. This figure does not include a federal interest-free loan of $12 million in 1969, and a further DIP grant of $10.6 million in 1971. In the same period Northern Electric and its subsidiaries paid $13.8 million in income tax. The public lost $10 million, while the company made a profit of $53.8 million.

You may think that perhaps the grants to the Bell complex created or, at the very least, preserved jobs. But no. Northern Electric's employment in Canada dropped from 21,694 in January 1971 to 16,951 in June 1972.

Particularly disturbing are the grants to Northern Electric and Microsystems International. These companies are owned 100 per cent by Mother Bell, according to the federal government's own statistics on intercorporate ownership. Now, you may feel that Mother Bell is wealthy enough to provide for her own offspring. You are right. In the last ten years Bell Canada has made over one billion dollars in net profits. Much of the credit must go to the "independent" Canadian Transport

Commission (the former chairman was Jack Pickersgill) which has consistently allowed Bell to jack up *your* telephone rates. With Edgar Benson now in charge of the commission, Bell's profits (and your telephone rates) will no doubt be going up again. Clearly, the government is letting Bell's fingers do the walking through the pockets of Canadians.

PAIT

In 1965 the Department of Industry, Trade and Commerce added to its network of grants to industry by announcing the Program of the Advancement of Industrial Technology (PAIT).

The purpose of PAIT is quite simple. PAIT is intended to promote growth and efficiency of industry in Canada by providing financial assistance to developmental projects. At first, program expenditures were quite modest, only $428,218 in the fiscal year 1965–1966. Five years later, expenditures had risen to $13 million. Last year the government allocated $26.7 million to the program, and Mr. Pépin expects to spend over $36 million in the current year, making a total of $97 million since the beginning of the program.

Here is the PAIT Honours List:

	$ million	1965–1966 to 1970–1971 % of total grants
1. Canadair Ltd.	5.2	15.2
2. Control Data Canada	1.9	5.7
3. Lockheed Offshore Petroleum Ltd.	1.7	5.1
4. Canadian General Electric	1.5	4.5
5. Noranda Mines	1.1	3.4
6. CAE Industries	0.8	2.4
7. Canadian Westinghouse	0.6	1.8
8. Textron Canada Ltd.	0.6	1.8
9. Canadian Cane Equipment	0.6	1.7
10. Leigh Instrument Ltd.	0.5	1.4
Total	14.7	43.0

Two of the companies, Canadair and CAE, also appear on the DIP Honours List.

The case of Control Data Canada Ltd. (a wholly owned subsidiary of its US parent company) is truly remarkable. In August 1970, DREE Minister Jean Marchand reported to Parliament that the company accepted an offer under RDIA of $4,106,715 to build a new plant in his hometown, aimed at creating 560 new jobs. But something went wrong. The RDIA grant was never paid. Instead, Control Data accepted an offer of a PAIT grant from Mr. Pépin in the amount of $19.3 million, with a cash advance of $1.9 million paid in the fiscal year 1970–1971. Some may prefer to call such manoeuvring an example of co-ordination in the federal cabinet; I prefer to call it an example of healthy competition in the cabinet. Did this US corporation need our tax money? In the last three years it has cleared $82 million in profits.

What about the Canadian General Electric grant? Was it necessary? The company's latest annual report suggests not. In the last five years CGE made profits of $71 million and paid taxes of just 12.6 per cent on its net earnings. It would appear that the company has ample resources of its own to invest. Perhaps you are thinking that the grant was necessary to create jobs. That is not the case. Between 1970 and 1971, the company's payroll dropped from 19,789 to 17,950, or a 10.2 per cent decrease.

The story is not yet complete. In addition to the $1.5 million grant under PAIT, the federal treasury helped out the company with $5.0 million under the Area Development Incentives Act (ADIA), $2.0 million in duty and tariff remissions, and $5,559 from DIP. Moreover, the company benefitted from the $4.9 million in federal grants given to shipyards for the purpose of building ships for General Electric.

Another well-known Canadian child of a US corporation, Canadian Westinghouse, received only $629,620 under PAIT. But other federal programs assisted the company to make a living in Canada. RDIA and DIP helped a bit, as did a forgiveable loan of $250,000 from Ontario. Total grants to this company between 1965–1966 and 1970–1971 amounted to $3.7 million. The grants were supplemented by fifteen remissions of customs and excise duty totalling $364,000.

In the same period the company paid $16.7 million income tax, or 21.2 per cent on net earnings of $79 million. After subtracting the dole from the governments, the company's income-tax rate was just 15.9 per cent, the same rate paid by a married taxpayer with two children and an annual income of $9300.

IRDIA

Mr. Pépin's department administers yet another research and development grant scheme, the Industrial Research and Development Incentives (IRDIA) program.

When this program began in 1967–1968, the annual expenditure was only $2.1 million. Over the next three years it rose to $30.1 million annually. Total IRDIA expenditure by the end of the current year will total close to $138 million.

The objective of this give-away program is "to induce Canadian corporations to undertake additional research and development likely to result in economic benefit to Canada." How this differs from the objective of PAIT is difficult to see, but there is one crucial difference between the two programs. Unlike PAIT expenditures, IRDIA grants are kept secret; the government refuses to make public the names of the companies receiving grants.

The excuse given by the government is the need for commercial secrecy. Mr. Pépin must feel that disclosure of the IRDIA grants would yield some sort of advantage to the recipients' competitors. It is difficult to assess the validity of the government's position, but if it is valid, why does a similar argument not apply in the case of PAIT? It is surprising that Mr. Pépin permits the disclosure of grants to the defence industry while concealing the names of firms receiving grants to develop goods for peaceful purposes.

The impact of IRDIA and other federal handouts on the stimulation of research and development is, to say the least, questionable. Employment in private research and development laboratories in Canada has been static since 1968, in spite of DIP, PAIT, IRDIA and all the other corporate welfare schemes. Furthermore, according to the Science Council of Canada, these laboratories are not expected to hire more than 300 university graduates annually—hardly enough to replace those people who leave them—a dismal proportion of the 14,000 science and engineering graduates being turned out each year by Canadian universities.

As a Canadian Senate committee reported last January,

"There is clearly something wrong with the government approach to the support of research and development and innovation in industry." The same committee reported that "Canada has the most elaborate system of grants to industry among all advanced countries." In other words, corporate welfare is more highly developed in Canada than in any other Western nation.

MACH

The Canadian tariff regulations provide for customs duties on most imported goods from abroad. If a Canadian spends a long weekend in the United States, he must pay duty for the clothes he might buy for his family there. This is normal and grudgingly accepted by all of us for the common good of our domestic economy.

Corporations, however, have been treated differently since 1968. Under the Machinery Remission Program (MACH), their machinery, accessories, attachments, control equipment, tools and components purchased abroad now receive a special consideration in that the government remits to the user all customs duty paid on such items.

This special consideration given to the corporations is not a pittance. In the last four years the federal treasury returned to the corporations $171 million. In some cases these concessions no doubt are warranted, especially when a particular piece of machinery cannot readily be produced in Canada.

However, an examination of the long lists in the public accounts suggests that in some cases the purpose of this program has been twisted. The stand-out example is Canadian Pacific Airlines. In 1968–1969 CP Air received from Ottawa a cheque of $5,156,439 in duties, sales and excise taxes remitted on aircraft and parts purchased abroad, with the explanation that these planes are used on international flights. Why does the government reward CP Air for buying their equipment abroad while at the same time it is lavishing millions of dollars upon the aircraft industry in Canada in a desperate effort to keep it afloat?

PEP

Research and development is one thing. But as far as the Ottawa bureaucracy is concerned, research into methods to increase productivity is an entirely separate matter.

Last year another grant program was begun in Mr. Pépin's department, the Program to Enhance Productivity (PEP). The amount allocated in the first year was small, just $500,000. But if the trends in PAIT and IRDIA expenditures are any indication, PEP will soon be another multimillion-dollar bonanza.

BEAM

In the minds of the Ottawa bureaucracy, productivity in general must be kept apart, if not in concept, at least in federal accounts, from productivity in the construction industry.

Mr. Pépin has a special fund for the construction industry under the Building Equipment, Accessories and Material (BEAM) program. There is just a few hundred thousand dollars there, but it is worth one's while to send in an application form.

IDAP

For some reason Mr. Pépin's department has seen fit to separate grants for product development from grants for product design. This device has given it the opportunity to set up yet one more give-away scheme, the Industrial Design Assistance Program (IDAP).

The expenditure, by federal give-away standards, is not overwhelming—only $2.3 million to date. But there is hope. A mere $42,000 was spent in 1970–1971; but the government has earmarked $1.5 million for the current fiscal year.

PIDA

This program, Pharmaceutical Industry Development Assistance (PIDA), dreamed up in 1968 by the Department of Industry, Trade and Commerce, is intended to improve the efficiency of the drug-manufacturing industry in Canada. Since this industry is 92 per cent foreign controlled, and since the grants are "neutral" about the nationality of recipient corporations, the program can be viewed as a veiled bribe to foreign manufacturers to switch their research and development efforts to branch plants in Canada.

The foreign corporations have chosen not to bite. The program has an annual budget of $2 million for loans and a lesser amount for direct grants. To date only six companies have applied for loans. Obviously, the parent corporations abroad are not prepared to shift their research and development efforts to Canada.

GAAP

As a result of the outcome of the Kennedy Round Agreements which resulted in a general reduction of tariffs, the Department of Industry, Trade and Commerce set up a new system of financial assistance to companies affected by "the new trading environment," the General Adjustment Assistance Program (GAAP).

The department may insure medium- and long-term loans up to a total of $250 million; it can give direct loans; or, finally, it can give grants towards the costs of consultants' fees.

To date the department has given away $254,000 in grants and $60 million in loans. No list of the recipients has been made public.

ESP

Shortly after President Nixon stunned his friends in Ottawa by announcing an import surcharge in August 1971, the federal government rushed through Parliament a bill to compensate manufacturers for loss of export orders. In this way it was hoped to protect Canadian jobs. The Employment Support Program (ESP) has been suspect from the beginning because grants were given to corporations with no reasonable guarantees about employment levels being required.

By the spring of this year, the government had disbursed $10.7 million. However, it refused to make public the names of the beneficiaries. As a result it is not known how many US-owned subsidiaries in Canada benefitted from Canadian government handouts, handouts prompted by the Nixon doctrine, which eventually returned to parent corporations in the United States.

AAA

Lest I give the impression that I condemn out of hand all programs of government assistance to industry, let me briefly discuss the Automotive Adjustment Assistance (AAA) program. The Canada-US Agreement on Automotive Products, signed in 1965, has been of great benefit to the automotive industry in Canada. However, as a result of the rationalization in the industry resulting from the auto pact, a number of auto parts manufacturers in Canada find themselves in grave difficulties. The government stepped in by providing loans under the AAA program. To date it has lent $92.5 million to 107 firms. This sort of government assistance to industry is logical and necessary to assist the industry during the transition period.

The above list does not exhaust the slate of programs administered by Mr. Pépin's department. There are many more. One, the Fashion Design Assistance Program, was announced with some fanfare by Mr. Pépin in April 1970.

Let us turn to the efforts of other federal government agencies in the field of corporate welfare.

IRAP

The Industrial Research Assistance Program (IRAP), shares with IRDIA the avowed purpose of "stimulating the interest of Canadian industry in research and development." This one, however, is administered by the National Research Council.

It is a more modest extravaganza than the competing IRDIA of the Department of Industry, Trade and Commerce: in the last seven years IRAP has given away "only" $37 million.

The relatively minor expenditure of this program may explain why the NRC is less secretive about who is on the dole. As you might suspect, the list includes the names of some of our best-known corporate citizens. For example, leading the Honours List are: Canadian General Electric ($2.1 million); MacMillan-Bloedel ($1.8 million); and Canadian Westinghouse ($1.6 million).

EGMA

Parliament passed the Emergency Gold-Mining Assistance (EGMA) Act in 1948 to provide financial help to marginally efficient gold mines facing fixed world prices for gold. Since that time, the federal government has spent some $289 million in direct subsidies to the industry. The program has been helpful to small gold mines during lean years, particularly in northern Ontario.

Originally, the program was intended as an emergency measure until more permanent steps could be taken to improve the plight of gold-mining communities. It is clear that successive governments have failed to solve the problem. From time to time the government serves notice on the gold-mining communities that it does not intend to do anything lasting for them. Instead, the "emergency" program is extended. The minister of Energy, Mines and Resources, only a few days before the call of this year's federal election, announced that the emergency measure will be extended for another few years.

The prospect for the gold-mining communities is not a good one, although the mining companies continue to make profits as long as the gold and the subsidies last. For instance, although Dome Mines Ltd. declared operating losses every year from 1966 to 1971, it was in actual fact able to show net profits for that period in the amount of $20.6 million. The federal subsidy of $8 million helped considerably. The remaining profits came from subsidiary and other dividends and interest. For all these profits and the federal subsidies, the company returned to the public treasury $995,000 income tax; that is, just 4.5 per cent of the company's net earnings of $22.1 million.

DIR

This plan, the Defence Industrial Research (DIR) program, must not be confused with DIP. The latter is within the jurisdiction of the Department of Industry, Trade and Commerce, whereas this program is under the Defence Research Board. Nevertheless, the objectives are the same.

Like most other members of the Alphabet Soup, this program involves outright grants to private industry. From the beginning of the program in 1962 until the current fiscal year, the handouts have amounted to $44 million. The top ten recipients for the period between 1965 and 1969 were:

	$ million	1965–1966 to 1969–1970 % of total grants
1. Northern Electric (subsidiary of Bell Canada)	3.7	16.1
2. Hawker-Siddeley complex in Canada (De Havilland Aircraft and Orenda Ltd.)	2.9	12.6
3. United Aircraft of Canada	1.8	8.0
4. Peace River Mining and Smelting	1.2	5.7
5. RCA Ltd.	1.0	4.4
6. Canadian General Electric	0.8	3.3
7. Litton Systems	0.7	3.1
8. Canadair Ltd.	0.7	2.9
9. Bomar Canada	0.6	2.8
10. Canadian Westinghouse	0.6	2.8
Total	14.0	61.2

Six of the ten members of the DIR Honours List are also found on the lists of DIP or PAIT. Canadair is found on all three lists. The executives never miss a handout.

ACCA

With good reason Canadians are concerned about their deteriorating environment. Almost predictably, the federal government's response has been to initiate yet one more program of corporate welfare. Environment Minister Jack Davis has threatened to make the polluters pay. And so they do, but tax concessions have eased the pain.

Companies are allowed to write off in only two years (straight-line depreciation) the total cost of pollution-control structures and equipment. As in all other cases of rapid write-offs, the result is deferred taxes.

In this short book there is scarcely room to discuss the many provincial versions of corporate welfare. It is enough to say that under free-enterprise governments in Canada, at any level, corporations do not have to look very hard for whatever kind of financial assistance they might want.

The same cannot be said for ordinary working Canadians. On September 21 of this year, the federal government announced that eighty investigators were being hired to track down possible violators of unemployment-insurance benefits.

The minister of Regional Economic Expansion, Jean Marchand, has not been nearly so concerned about possible violations in connection with RDIA grants. Although NDP members of Parliament have been pressing him for many months to investigate claims of irregularities, and have been urging him to present an evaluation of the results of his give-away program, Mr. Marchand has persisted in ignoring the evidence before his eyes.

With flocks of lawyers and accountants to protect their interests, our corporate welfare bums need not lose much sleep. The ordinary man has no such guardians; all he has is a hungry family and a pile of bills to pay.

We can be reasonably certain that several unemployed people who, out of desperation, have cheated the government of a few hundred dollars, will be tracked down and punished.

And we can be equally certain that the government will continue to overlook flagrant abuses of the corporate welfare system, and will continue to disburse hundreds of millions of the taxpayers' dollars in the most totally disorganized and haphazard manner possible.

Reprinted with permission of the *Ottawa Citizen*

Federal Grants—Incentives to Industry
$ million

	1965	1966	1967	1968	1969	1970	1971	1972	Total 1965–1972
				Fiscal year beginning in					
Dept. of Industry, Trade & Commerce									
AAA	—	—	0.6	2.7	3.4	0.9	N/A	N/A	7.6
BEAM	—	—	—	—	—	0.2	0.1	0.1	0.4
CASE	—	—	—	—	—	—	—	0.5	0.5
DMC	—	—	—	—	—	—	—	0.2	0.2
DIP	26.8	30.8	33.5	29.6	48.5	45.2	42.3	43.5	300.2
ESP	—	—	—	—	—	—	10.7	—	10.7
EMD	—	—	—	—	—	—	1.0	3.7	4.7
GAAP	—	—	—	x	0.1	x	0.5	0.5	1.1
MVM	8.1	2.6	2.6	111.3	75.7	2.7	N/A	N/A	203.0
IDAP	—	—	—	—	—	x	0.8	1.5	2.3
IRDIA	—	—	2.1	19.6	23.0	30.1	31.0	32.0	137.8
MACH	—	—	5.3	39.1	55.2	71.5	80.0*	85.0*	336.1
PEP	—	—	—	—	—	x	0.5	0.5	1.0
PAIT	0.4	4.6	6.4	4.3	5.3	13.1	26.7	36.4	97.2
SCSP	40.5	35.8	39.3	22.3	14.2	13.7	20.5	26.5	212.8
Dept. of Environment									
ACCA	—	—	—	—	—	—	87.0*	120.0*	207.0*
Dept. of Energy, Mines & Resources									
CCEA	134.6	82.3	71.6	—	—	—	—	—	288.5
SCT	22.5	37.8	33.4	7.0	8.6	6.0	4.1	4.1	123.5
EGM	14.8	15.0	15.2	14.7	13.7	13.1	14.5	14.2	115.2

	1965	1966	1967	Fiscal year beginning in 1968	1969	1970	1971	1972	Total 1965–1972
Dept. of Indian Affairs & Northern Development									
NMEAP	—	—	2.8	4.1	5.0	0.2	1.6	—	13.7
PAP	x	—	x	x	x	x	0.1	0.1	0.2
Dept. of Regional Economic Expansion									
ADIA	—	1.2	15.4	14.6	54.5	47.4	63.1	22.7	218.9
RDIA	—	—	—	—	—	12.9	36.3	147.3	196.5
Defence Research Board									
DIR	5.3	4.7	4.5	4.3	4.0	4.5	4.5	4.5	36.3
National Research Council									
IRAP	3.3	4.2	4.2	5.1	6.3	6.9	7.4	8.4	45.8
Dept. of Transport									
TS	118.4	147.1	153.5	122.2	123.1	110.8	83.7	72.6	931.4
Total	374.7	366.1	390.4	400.9	440.6	379.2	516.4	624.3	3,490.6

SOURCE: For the years 1965 to 1970 — Public Accounts of Canada
For the years 1971 and 1972 — Estimates of the Government of Canada

* Estimate
x Less than $50,000

AAA — Automotive Adjustment Assistance Program

ACCA — Accelerated Capital Cost Allowance Program

ADIA — Area Development Incentives Act

BEAM — Building Equipment, Accessories & Materials Program

CASE — Counselling Assistance to Small Enterprises

CCEA — Canadian Coal Equality Act

DMC — Development of Management Courses

DIP — Defence Industry Productivity Program

DIR — Defence Industrial Research Program

EGM — Emergency Gold-Mining Assistance Program

EMD — Program for Export Market Development

ESP — Employment Support Program

GAAP — General Adjustment Assistance Program

IDAP — Industrial Design Assistance Program

IRAP — Industrial Research Assistance Program

IRDIA — Industrial Research & Development Incentives Act

MACH — Machinery Program

MVM — Motor Vehicle Manufacturers' Remission

NMEAP — Northern Mineral Exploration Assistance Program

PAIT — Program for the Advancement of Industrial Technology

PAP — Prospectors Assistance Program

PEP — Program to Enhance Productivity

RDIA — Regional Development Incentives Act

SCSP — Ship Construction Subsidy Program

SCT — Subventions for Coal Transport

TS — Transport Subsidies

The above is just a brief sketch of Ottawa's grant jungle. I doubt that there is a single person in the Ottawa bureaucracy (certainly not in the cabinet) who is fully aware of all the possibilities. As my own personal contribution to corporate welfare, perhaps I can point out to any interested person in the business community the best path to follow through this maze.

Suppose you are the president of a reasonably well-to-do manufacturing establishment in one of Canada's "have" provinces. Your profits are satisfactory, but there are clouds on the horizon. The provincial government is after you to install some expensive new piece of anti-pollution equipment. The union local in your plant is demanding job security and a wage hike which would bring them in line with other employees in the industry. You begin to consider relocating in a low-wage area where the anti-pollution regulations are not quite so stringent.

How do you proceed? You first make discreet enquiries of business associations in other provinces. No doubt you will find that the grass can be very much greener on the other side. Suppose that you uncover two prospective areas where you could relocate. Both are so-called "designated" areas. You then check with the local politicians to ensure that pollution standards will not prove to be a problem. At the same time you make a few discreet enquiries about the attitude of the local politicians towards organized labour, just in case.

Having obtained this pertinent information you indicate to both provincial governments your interest in relocation. They will likely respond with alacrity. At this point you must play one province against the other in order to obtain the best possible bargain for yourself. Among other concessions, you can hope to win in this process: exemption from municipal taxes and land-use regulations, guaranteed power and water at a price well below the market rate, interest-free loans, and perhaps even an outright grant. Choose the better bargain.

Now you get serious. You go to Ottawa.

The best starting point for entering the Ottawa corporate welfare maze is the Department of Regional Economic Expansion (DREE). You need not hide the fact that your company is a wholly owned subsidiary of a prosperous and well-known foreign corporation. Federal bureaucrats are impressed by that sort of thing.

There are several strategies you may use at this level. For instance, one gambit, which has been successful for some companies, is to suggest that your company is actively considering relocation and that you think that a foreign country would be your best choice. Or you may say that your company intends eventually to expand its production facilities into other parts of Canada, that with some public "assistance" you might find it possible to locate forthwith in a designated area.

Be prepared for reams of red tape. Do not let it deter you. There is only one piece of information that is of importance to the DREE bureaucrats: how much you want.

Above all, do not be modest. Remember that the importance of a DREE grant to the politicians in power is not so much what it does for the designated area, but what it does for the government's popularity. There is a great deal of political hay to be made from the announcement of a multimillion-dollar grant which promises to help create several hundred jobs. There is virtually no political punch in the announcement of a grant of less than one million dollars. Therefore, it is important that you exaggerate your requirements.

The legislation governing DREE grants requires that they conform to certain standards. The size of the handouts you receive must be related to the number of jobs that you claim will be created and to the amount of capital that you claim you will invest yourself. Leave the calculations to the DREE officials; they have become very proficient in the last year or so.

So far, if you have been a smart operator, you will have assembled municipal, provincial and federal assistance. But don't stop now; the game is just warming up.

The path to follow from this point depends upon the type of industry you are engaged in.

Suppose you manufacture electronic components. Start with DIP. You will be required to demonstrate some potential for engaging in the international armaments industry, which is not as difficult as it might at first appear. All kinds of companies located in Canada have received DIP handouts. For example, Donald Ropes and Wire Cloth Ltd., and even Long Sault Woodcraft Ltd., were offered DIP grants.

A strong bargaining tactic to use when dealing with the Ottawa mandarins is to let it be known that your company is engaged in "original research," or could become so with a bit of federal assistance. If you are able to dress up a part of your planned operations as "research" ("research and development" is even better), you might find it profitable to visit the DIR bureaucracy.

Of course, not all industries can present themselves as participants in the defence effort. If your intended product is a clearly civilian one, you must pass up DIP and DIR. Don't be concerned. Cases like yours are provided for.

As a manufacturer of non-military equipment, an excellent point of entry into the corporate welfare maze is PAIT. You will be asked to show that the project you have in mind is of a developmental nature. This should not be difficult. All sorts of companies, from the Canadian Lady Corset Company to Crescent Cheese Company, have managed to convince Ottawa that their operations were adding to the advancement of Canadian industrial technology. Another program to investigate is IRDIA. To this set of bureaucrats you have to demonstrate that your planned research operations are "additional" to your present research operations and will "likely result in economic benefit to Canada." I do not know how PAIT and IRDIA differ but neither, I suspect, do their administrators. Your opportunities in this classic bureaucratic situation can be truly golden.

But the possibilities for an industry with a "research" angle are not yet exhausted. Another R&D give-away program, IRAP, is available to an enterprising corporate manager. IRAP is charged with "stimulating the interest of Canadian industry in research and development." Whose interest would not be stimulated when the rewards are considered?

As a successful corporate manager you will be well aware of the importance of eye-catching design in ensuring market success. The federal government is too. It offers you yet another service, IDAP, a program to help you put your product in a pretty package.

If your parent company or its subsidiaries abroad are interested in selling you the equipment for the new plant, accommodate them. Your purchasing department can certainly write the specifications in such a way that no company in Canada can honestly claim they can supply it readily. However, purchasing abroad does not cost you any more than buying Canadian would. Under MACH, the federal government will happily remit to you all customs duty.

In case you are thinking that the maze game has been exaggerated here, let me quote you the words of Jean Des Rosiers, president of La Chambre de Commerce du District de Montréal, as reported in the *Globe and Mail* business section on September 22, 1972:

> ... by laziness, conservatism and letting things go, they [top management] will wind up qualifying for grants to maintain competitiveness artificially; other grants under the category [of] new-job creation to take on again personnel they laid off six months earlier; still more grants every time they threaten to close down.

Let me remind you that grants are not the only type of corporate welfare available from the federal government. There is the bonanza available to the enterprising corporation through the tax system. Corporations in the natural-resource sector and land developers are well aware of the advantages for them in this area. However, as a means of delivering corporate welfare, the tax system has one significant advantage over the grant mechanism. Most grants are highly visible; tax concessions are not. Corporations particularly susceptible to public criticism (e.g., large, foreign-owned corporations which export Canada's natural resources in an unprocessed state) will find it in their interest to receive corporate welfare through the tax system rather than through grants.

CHAPTER SEVEN

Participatory Tax Reform

Tax reform would not be an issue today if the tax system had truly been reformed in 1971–1972. Since it took almost ten years to accomplish the little reform there was, all the greater is the tragedy.

In 1962 the Diefenbaker government set up the Royal Commission on Taxation. The terms of reference set out in the order-in-council creating it are worth noting. The commission was instructed to:

> ... inquire into and report upon the incidence and effects of taxation imposed by Parliament, including any changes made during the currency of the inquiry, upon the operation of the national economy, the conduct of business, the organization of industry and the positions of individuals; and to make recommendations for improvements in the tax laws and their administration that may be consistent with the maintenance of a sufficient flow of revenue; and without restricting the generality of the foregoing, the Commission shall consider and report upon:
>
> a) the distribution of burdens among taxpayers resulting from existing rates, exemptions, reliefs and allowances provided in the personal and corporation income taxes, estate taxes and sales and excise taxes, taking into account also the jurisdiction and practices of the provinces and municipalities;
> b) the effects of the tax system on employment, living standards, savings and investment, industrial productivity, and economic stability and growth;
> c) provisions in existing laws which may have given rise over the years to anomalies or inequities or which may require action to close loopholes which permit the use of devices to avoid fair taxation;
> d) the effects of the income, sales and excise taxes and estate duties on income and investment flows which affect the balance of international payments and economic relations with other countries;

e) the means whereby the tax laws can best be formulated to encourage Canadian ownership of Canadian industry without discouraging the flow of investment funds into Canada;

f) the changes that may be made to achieve greater clarity, simplicity and effectiveness in the tax laws or their administration; and

g) such other related matters as the Commissioners consider pertinent or relevant to the specific or general scope of the inquiry.

With these instructions the commission began the most extensive review of a nation's tax system ever undertaken.

The *Report* of the Royal Commission on Taxation, finally published in February 1967, showed that the commissioners had arrived at some startling conclusions:

1. The present system does not afford fair treatment for all Canadians. People in essentially similar circumstances do not bear the same taxes. People in essentially different circumstances do not bear appropriately different tax burdens.

2. Canadians are less well off than they could be because there are fewer goods and services available than could be provided with the more efficient use of labour, capital and natural resources. The present tax system has contributed to this unfortunate result in two ways:

a) It needlessly distorts the distribution of productive goods and services.

b) It fails to compensate where it could for some non-tax barriers to the efficient allocation of productive goods and services.

3. The fiscal system has not been used as effectively as it could have been used to maintain full employment, contain inflationary increases in the price level, and encourage Canadian ownership and control of Canadian industry.

4. In some tax fields compliance and collection costs have been needlessly raised because of duplicate federal and provincial administrations.

5. Federal tax administration is not sufficiently shielded from political influence and is too centralized for efficiency and convenience.

6. Federal procedures used to obtain and analyze new ideas prior to the introduction of new federal tax legisla-

tion are inadequate, as are the procedures for hearing the views of taxpayers and other interested parties on proposed legislation.

7. Federal administrative and judicial appeal procedures are deficient and require reforms.

Leading academics sang its praises. Richard Musgrave, a renowned scholar of taxation, was moved to near poetry in his comment on the report in the *Canadian Tax Journal*:

> ... its sheer monumentality and structural logic tower over the reviewer. The spire of vertical equity reaches into the heavens of non-discretionary income; the nave of horizontal equity is sweeping in its purity of accretion, and the transcepts of constructive realization and integration complete the unity of the Simonesque design.*

Others were less moved to praise, although their comments were not much easier to understand than Musgrave's: Montreal lawyer Philip Vineberg described the report as "too logical" (*Montreal Gazette,* November 28, 1967).

The greatest opposition came from the mining and oil industry. A *Globe & Mail* editorial (May 27, 1967) noted that:

> ... among the more courageous deeds of the Royal Commission on Taxation was that it said out loud that there are certain industries in our midst that have not been carrying their fair share of taxation and that this inequality should be corrected.
>
> The courage, in fact, may verge on foolhardiness for the industries thus assailed are among the most powerful and entrenched in the country ...

Within a few weeks after the publication of the report the minister of Finance, Mitchell Sharp, had already promised the oil and mining industry that the three-year tax holiday on new mines would not end before 1971 (not before 1976 in the present legislation).

This was only the beginning of a parade of concessions to powerful vested interests. Deadline after deadline passed as the country waited for the government to declare its position.

The provincial premiers' objections voiced in June and July of 1967, the Liberal leadership race beginning in December

---

*July–August 1967, p. 349.

1967, the defeat of the mini-budget tax bill in February of 1968, the Honourable E. J. Benson replaced Mitchell Sharp as minister of Finance to take charge of tax reform.

Benson wanted to avoid a white paper, and so he began by going directly to legislation. In the October 22, 1968 budget, proposals which more or less coincided with the recommendations of the Royal Commission on Taxation were introduced that would tax insurance companies and reduce tax-free transfers within financial institutions. However, he proposed changes in the estate and gift taxes which rejected the Carter commission position.

> While respecting the intellectual coherence and elegance of the case made by the Royal Commission on Taxation on this matter—crudely summed up in the phrase that "a buck is a buck is a buck"—I believe that the overwhelming weight of Canadian opinion is against it now ...

Clearly, the government had no intention of being criticized on the grounds of being "too logical."

Mr. Benson's assessment of the weight of public opinion was itself overwhelmed by the cries of protest that rose in opposition to the estate-tax bill.

In a quieter way, insurance companies were "consulting" with the government about their tax situation. In April 1969 1968 and the Canadian dollar crisis in March of 1968 all served to delay government administration on tax reform. Early in the insurance companies were able to welcome softer, revised proposals from the government.

In the meantime it had become apparent that the Department of Justice could not produce a draft bill before the summer recess, so the white paper idea was revived with a June target (*Financial Times,* September 8, 1969.)

In the June 1969 budget, the target for publication of the white paper was announced as sometime during the summer recess. Finally, in November 1969, the white paper was released.

The release of the white paper was like the first offer in a complex negotiation. The stakes were the tax privileges of the vested interests and the income level of every Canadian.

The white paper was a great disappointment, after the prolonged, but in many respects constructive debate that followed publication of the Carter report. Essentially, it maintained the tax structure that had prompted the establishment of the Carter commission in the first place.

After a debate in the House of Commons the white paper was referred to the Standing Committee on Trade, Finance and Economic Affairs, where the lobbying began in earnest.

A total of 213 presentations were made to the committee; 68 per cent of them were either by individual corporations or by corporate-interest groups such as the Canadian Manufacturing Association.

Witnesses Appearing before the Committee

	No.	Percentage
1. Individual Companies (Mining, Manufacturing, Utilities, Financial, etc.)	68	32
2. Industrial, Commercial and Financial Associations	76	35
3. Agricultural Associations	7	3
4. Labour and Employee Associations	5	2
5. Educational, Cultural and Charitable Associations	20	10
6. Professional Associations (Lawyers, Doctors, Engineers, Architects, etc.)	23	11
7. Individuals	8	4
8. Others (mainly governments)	6	3
Total	213	100

Among the companies that submitted briefs were some familiar names: Alcan, Bell Canada, Brinco, Cadillac Development Co., Imperial Oil, Denison Mines, INCO, National Sea Products, Shell Canada Ltd. and Stelco, among others.

Their indignation about the white paper proposals was almost enough to convince the most sceptical that they were actually major taxpayers.

The committee hearings dragged on through the winter of 1969–70 into the summer of 1970.

Towards the end of July 1970, the committee divided into two sub-committees, one of which travelled east and the other west to hold hearings across the country. On October 5, 1970, the committee presented its report to the House of Commons and the vested interests registered another victory.

The authors of the committee report did not need to fear that their product would be scorned by businessmen as "too logical."

> ... a number of the committee's suggestions for modifying White Paper proposals stem not from a belief that proposals are inequitable or detrimental to economic growth, but from a concern for taxpayer understanding and acceptance.
>
> The Committee is of the opinion that its recommendations, if implemented, would promote the equity emphasized in the White Paper and at the same time eliminate any possible bias against economic growth which some Canadians feared would be a by-product in their original form.
>
> The Committee believes, therefore, that its recommendations will meet with general approval as a reasonable basis for building a fairer tax system.*

But the committee had already stated that equity or "fairness" is in the eyes of the beholder.

> We have seen taxpayers who would face increased tax burdens under the proposals reason that because the proposals would have an adverse economic impact on them or their activities, there would be an equal or even greater adverse economic impact on the whole private sector of the economy. That this attitude was sometimes carried to extremes and even dramatized to the point of destroying credibility does not alter the fact that it exists.**

Here we come precisely to the point: other attitudes exist too. The attitude of the majority of Canadians who stood to benefit from the proposals that the committee rejected was not adequately taken into consideration.

---

*Canada, Standing Committee on Finance, Trade and Economic Affairs, *Report Respecting the White Paper on Tax Reform* (Ottawa, October 1970), p. 11.
**p. 10.

Ordinary taxpayers are not in a position to hire experts to inform them in specific terms which aspects of the proposed change are beneficial and which are harmful to their interests. They are not in a position to have sophisticated briefs prepared, nor are they, generally, in a position to take the time and trouble to present the briefs to finance ministers or parliamentary committees.

All of these things can be done by corporate taxpayers because these expenditures are deductible and because they have the resources to spend.

Finally, if the original proposals are considered to be of benefit to the ordinary taxpayer, why should he spend money defending them? Interests that are threatened by the original proposals have a clear and specific purpose in removing that threat.

And in the final analysis they did. When the draft of Bill C-259 was presented to the House of Commons on Friday, June 18, 1971, Bay Street breathed a collective sigh.

CHAPTER EIGHT

Beyond the Corporate Welfare State

Within the last twenty years or so we have built in Canada what I have described as the corporate welfare state. In the preceding chapters of this brief book I have barely explored the edges of the complex inter-relationship between government and the corporate sector. There is so much more to discover.

The corporate welfare state seems to have begun in the late forties as governments attempted to face the trauma of turning the economy from war production to peacetime production without the major economic crises that followed the First World War.

From its humble beginnings it grew into a system of grants and tax concessions of massive proportions. The growth of the corporate welfare state derived from an approach to economic development which worships at the Shrine of the Gross National Product. One ad hoc policy was piled on top of another. Each new government, and almost every new cabinet minister, added to the list of give-away programs, oblivious to what had been done before and probably unaware of what others were doing.

The system has become so complex and expensive that we must stop and ask what we are accomplishing.

The government itself does not evaluate the effectiveness of its programs. And anyone who asks questions is charged with being against whatever the programs are intended to achieve.

The critics of present regional-development policies are accused of being against regional development. Jean Marchand tells the premiers of the Atlantic provinces that if the criticism of the incentives grants to private industry continues, the money will be cut off. The prime minister is more credible. On September 16, 1972, he told his Halifax audience: "If people don't like them [regional-expansion grants] we'll give them all to Quebec." Opposition politicians are accused of being against the Maritimers or of being anti-Quebec.

Those who question the effectiveness of the government's

grants and tax concessions to the extractive industry are labelled by the minister of Finance as builders of ghost towns in northern Ontario. Those who ask about the shipbuilding subsidy are accused of intending to dismantle the shipbuilding industry.

This negative attitude is the best proof of the government's uneasiness that the system is not working. The government is conveniently forgetting that they are the trustees of *our* tax money. It is not enough to show in the public accounts that our money was disbursed according to the accepted accounting principles: the columns of revenues and expenditures may well add up, although the auditor-general gives us an annual glimpse of some strange additions. What concerns you and me is simply who is putting the money in, who is getting it out, and what good it does.

Whatever the government says about its achievements, we know that prices are going up, as are the numbers of unemployed; that as many Canadians are living below the poverty line now as twenty years ago; that regional disparities are just as pronounced as ever; that taxes for middle-income Canadians are increasing; that corporations are getting away with a smaller and smaller share of the tax burden and that their profits are getting bigger.

This is the result of the government's economic and fiscal policies and the grant strategy. No amount of promises to the needy at election time will make the wrong policies right; nor will it lessen the enormous price we have to pay for them.

If the programs, whatever they are, do not deliver, or at least do not come close to the target, they must be scrapped. The game of using successes in individual cases as proof of general achievement is a crude device of deception. Promises of better things to come, repeated for years and years, are a cruel hoax on those who are hoping and waiting.

The sizable grant handouts to corporations must be objectively examined to assess their contribution to the achievement of stated objectives. But many of the federal grants are secret, and the taxpayer who pays for them is left in complete ignorance. One grant system, the regional development incentives by DREE, is reasonably open. After three years of these handouts in full view of the public, the record is dismal. Outsiders punctured so many holes in that system that the minister

105

himself had to agree hurriedly to a thorough evaluation. The misfortune of Jean Marchand was that while he informed the public about the objective of each handout, the name of the lucky corporation and the amount involved, he forgot to examine whether or not the stated objectives were achieved.

Does it mean that the other grant systems are safe from public scrutiny? Until very recently that appeared to be the case. Many of them are protected in the name of commercial or public interest. Others give us amounts and names of the beneficiaries, but without stated objectives. The difference is really not significant. Nobody, including the ministers, really knows what was achieved, and never will.

Moreover, there is not a known case of prosecution against a recipient corporation for misrepresentation or misuse of government grants. You and I know of many cases where unemployed workers have been dragged into court for drawing ten or one hundred dollars more than the rules allowed.

Does this mean that all cases involving billions of dollars of grants to corporations were handled properly, to the letter? Hardly. But we will never know, nor will we ever get our money back.

However, we do know that the billions of dollars doled out to the corporations leave us with the same problems we had before the corporate welfare state was really launched.

The same is true of tax concessions to corporations, except that the process of finding out what tax concessions actually accomplish is much more complicated. On these grounds alone a good case can be made for doing away with them. Even the minister of Finance has admitted that the latest tax concessions contained in his maiden budget of last May will take some unspecified amount of time to "bite." ("Fraser Kelly Show," CFTO, September 16, 1972.)

We do know that neither tax concessions nor grants have achieved the results which their sponsors claimed for them. We do know that the hundreds of millions of dollars each year must come out of the heavy tax burden carried by the individual taxpayer.

Eric Kierans has detailed the history of the investment booms and busts that have regularly followed previous attempts to stimulate capital investment. Excessive investment in the private sector draws resources away from social needs. Housing in particular suffers as interest rates rise, with the result that we fall further behind in our efforts to provide the right kind of housing at the right price or rent to Canadians who desperately require decent shelter. The impact of the Turner budget on housing will be all the more critical since the number of young people who have arrived at the age of family formation is the fastest growing segment of our population.

The Turner budget proposals (the legislation enacting them into law has not yet been passed) continue and further contribute to the practice of making the cost of capital equipment relatively less expensive than labour. Businessmen will prefer to expand by techniques that employ machinery and equipment rather than labour. The supposedly job-creating tax concessions of Mr. Turner and his predecessors have the effect of decreasing rather than increasing the potential number of jobs.

Again, the number of young people reaching the age where they are looking for jobs—the right kind of jobs—has increased rapidly in the past few years. It will increase more rapidly in the next few years. In this context, it seems outrageous that the government could continue a system that so clearly reduces the chances of our young people to find the jobs for which they have been educated.

It is not that the government has not been told, and it is not that it does not understand. The Honourable Eric Kierans resigned from the cabinet because the government would not listen to his warnings about the perverse direction of our economic policy. The prime minister makes it clear that he not only listened, he understood and he agreed, but something else stood in the way. Mr. Trudeau put it this way: "Mr. Kierans's economic ideas I generally agree with—it's his politics I don't like." To do what Kierans wanted, according to the prime minister, "would have been courageous economics but bad politics." (September 10, 1971, Port Hope.)

Four years ago, Prime Minister Trudeau appeared to be in accord with Mr. Kierans, at least in one respect. On April 26, 1968, he said, according to the *Regina Leader Post*: "We need to specialize in the production of goods we believe we can make best. We must choose the areas of production which we believe will be of greatest importance to the world of tomorrow and then concentrate our energies and resources on these."

He was referring, as he frequently has, to the communications industry, one of the few industries in this country controlled by Canadian firms. Why then was a $21-million PAIT grant given to the foreign-owned Control Data, and an RDIA grant of $6 million given to the American-owned IBM? These grants cannot fail but help such giants of the communications industry wipe out their Canadian competition.

Mr. Kierans described a number of other distortions that result from the government's almost mystical belief in stimulating private investment.

Firms that rely more heavily on machinery for production than on labour are stuck with producing the kind of goods that the machines can produce. If the product becomes obsolete, the business is not in a position to change its production easily to something else. The cost of the new machines and the old tend to be added to the price of the products.

Excessive capital-cost allowances discriminate in favour of industries that rely heavily on investment and physical capital, and against industries like the service industry which employ people.

Incentives based on capital-cost allowances discriminate against new firms. Unless the firm is earning profits, which often takes a few years, the capital-cost allowances are worthless. Once the firm moves into a profitable position it then can charge all the capital-cost allowances it has saved up against income to avoid paying taxes for a few more years. The point is that existing firms, which are 47.7 per cent foreign owned, benefit and can use those benefits to prevent new competition.

Concessions reduce government revenues from the corporate sector, which means they must come from somewhere else. Invariably they come from the pay cheques of individual Canadian taxpayers.

In summary, the system of concessions to corporations contributes to the cycle of inflation followed by unemployment, bursts of house-building activity followed by shortages. After twenty years, no significant dent has been made in the problem of regional disparities. Yet the government continues to believe it is on the right course and that eventually the policies will "bite".

How can supposedly intelligent men continue to believe in what so clearly does not work?

H. S. Gordon, a Canadian economist known for his studies on the history of economic thought, reminds his students that the medical practitioners that poured incredible elixirs and potions made from frogs, snakes, rabbits' feet and a variety of herbs and spices down the throat of the dying King Charles II of England were the best medical minds of their day. They were behaving in what they believed to be a perfectly rational way, giving the King the best possible treatment. Nowadays, we view their approach as ridiculous, even laughable, but they believed in it and the practice continued for a long time.

It gives me no satisfaction to know that some future economic historians may view today's economic remedies with the same scorn that the medical profession has for the bleeding of patients and the application of leeches. A change in direction is urgently required.

I have previously referred to the growing numbers of persons in the twenty to thirty age bracket. As a result of the 1946–1962 post-war baby boom, we have already experienced classroom crowding in public schools, high schools and universities as this entirely predictable population source worked its way up the age ladder. Now the federal government is failing again to anticipate the type of demand that will be placed upon them by those who want to join the productive stream of our society.

The following table shows clearly the problems associated with the shifting importance of age in the Canadian population.

Age Composition of Canadian Population for Selected Age Groups

		1961	1966	1971	1976	1981	1984
15-19	No.	1,433	1,838	2,114	2,338	2,255	1,957
	%	(7.9)	(9.2)	(9.8)	(10.1)	(9.0)	(7.5)
20-24	No.	1,184	1,461	1,907	2,169	2,387	2,397
	%	(6.5)	(7.3)	(8.8)	(9.3)	(9.5)	(9.1)
25-29	No.	1,209	1,242	1,576	1,970	2,225	2,378
	%	(6.6)	(6.2)	(7.3)	(8.5)	(8.9)	(9.1)
30-34	No.	1,272	1,242	1,316	1,610	2,002	2,159
	%	(7.0)	(6.2)	(6.1)	(6.9)	(8.4)	(8.2)

SOURCE: Report to the Secretary of State by the Committee on Youth, p. 12.

It is perfectly clear now that the capacity of our economy to provide housing will be severely tested in the next ten years. The projections indicate that the absolute increase in the twenty to twenty-nine age bracket will be 1.3 million persons in the next twelve years.

The *Financial Times* of July 31, 1972, reported it this way:

> The baby-boom children are now approaching their mid-twenties. Many have married and have children of their own. As a result, far more people than usual are ready to buy their first house. This trend will continue well into the 1980s.

Housing is not the only pressure point that we can reasonably expect in the near future, although it is the most immediate. A wide range of government services will be tested by this population surge, including manpower programs and health services among others. Recreation, culture and sports, the leisure-time activities, will all demand greater government attention.

The most important, however, is the provision of meaningful jobs for this energetic group of Canadians who, through their education, are even better prepared for the world of work than those who are already in it. They will make demands on the economic system in terms of new goods and services from the private sector and better and more humane treatment from the public sector. But at the same time they are the very resources that can make it all happen. The government must be committed to making sure that their ideas for the future and their capacity to realize them will be able to meet tomorrow's challenges. It is my conviction that this can only be done if we move beyond the corporate welfare state.

The needs of our country and our people are undisputed. Even the Liberal government recognizes them in that it speaks about justice and the eradication of regional disparities. But Mr. Trudeau believes that private enterprise is the *main* vehicle to achieve these ends. Mr. Stanfield believes corporations are *essential* to the process of building our country.

I say it is the government's responsibility to do the job. Governments are elected by people; corporations are not. Governments must answer to the people; corporations must answer only to their boards.

For this reason I reject the solutions of the past. I oppose unbridled give-aways to corporations, programs without strategy, evaluation or fair returns to the people of Canada.

I believe that every Canadian has the right to share fairly in the wealth of our country, regardless of where he lives. But I emphatically do not believe that private enterprise alone can be relied upon to make these rights a reality. If it could, poverty and regional disparity would not have arisen in the first place.

Free enterprise has a role in our society. But its role must be in accord with the objectives of our people. Only where this role contributes to our well-being should we give encouragement through the use of public funds.

In the last eight years, the federal government gave away $3.5 billion to industry in the form of grants and other subsidies, and approximately twice as much in income-tax concessions—a total of $10 billion to the corporations, most of them large and wealthy. Despite all this corporate welfare, hundreds of thousands of Canadians are jobless, and millions are living in poverty. Messrs. Trudeau and Stanfield talk about the importance of "business confidence." With profits rising every year, I don't believe we have to cater any longer to this bromide. It is the confidence of ordinary Canadians, especially those people who have no jobs and no future, that concerns me. No matter what statistical trickery the government may choose to use, half a million people, and often more, are being sacrificed to the powerful gods of the free-enterprise myth. And millions more are squeezed by high taxes, high interest rates and the rising cost of food and shelter.

The government must stop its haphazard give-away programs. It must start with concrete and detailed objectives to develop a strategy.

A fair distribution of income should be the first and paramount goal. In this wealthy nation there is no reasonable excuse for poverty to ravage whole regions and whole segments of the population.

The present maze of corporate welfare programs undoubtedly arose piecemeal. It was not part of a grand design; it just happened. It happened because there was a highly favourable disposition to corporations on the part of government. But it happened also because the government had neither the imagination nor the courage to look for new solutions. Moreover, existing grant systems, too often contradictory and ineffective, are allowed to continue only because the cabinet minister administering the program is too powerful to be challenged. Old soldiers never die; old grant programs seldom fade away.

The resulting maze is a mess. What is most urgently needed is to clean it up. Every grant program must immediately be thoroughly and objectively evaluated. If it does not stand up to this scrutiny, it must be dropped.

Corporations that receive public grants should be accountable to the public. They need not be ashamed of being on the dole, provided they fulfil their obligations. If a corporation gets a million dollars from the federal treasury to put up a plant and create five hundred jobs in a region where jobs are scarce, the corporation must show that it is doing just that. If not, the money must be given back instead of ending up in the corporate profit column.

Government, like any other investor, should obtain equity in a given venture for its invested capital. If the corporation makes profits, the public purse should benefit. On the other hand, any losses should be carried by all shareholders, including government. Government's share in the control of the enterprise will help ensure that the corporation does not pull out ten years later, leaving the workers and the country holding the bag.

International corporate giants do not need our money, especially when we know that they will use it to expand their hold over the Canadian economy. Most certainly they should not benefit from public subsidies in any form, be they grants or tax concessions.

Government's financial help must be more intensively directed to those enterprises which are most capable of helping as many people as possible. There is no reason why our fishermen need an intermediary to process and market the fish they are catching. The business know-how can be purchased. The benefits from processing and distribution, which are much more substantial than from catching the fish, should be kept by those who contribute most, the fishermen.

Co-operatives must be given priority by public-assistance programs, not only for our fishermen but most certainly for our farmers. It is time the myth that working people are incapable of running a business be discarded. If food processors and distributors are capable of making a profit, so is the man

112

who grows the grain and catches the fish. And the consumer would benefit with fewer middlemen taking profits along the way.

The government must dare to go it alone in cases where private capital is unwilling to move in without large-scale handouts from the public treasury. Crown corporations are not only the most suitable instrument of achieving social goals in many areas; they are just as capable of competing in domestic and foreign markets as any private corporation.

The federal government can no longer afford to pretend it is the only government capable of developing solutions. It must be the leader, but it must also firmly understand that arrogance is not the same thing as leadership. Provinces, regions, and indeed municipalities, have just as much responsibility for the well-being of their population. They are better equipped to set their own priorities and objectives than are the bureaucrats in Ottawa. Without their contribution Canada will never become what it should be.

Taxation policies, like direct subsidies, must serve both economic and social goals. Tax concessions and loopholes must be eliminated. In principle they are unjust, and in practice they are ineffective as tools for desirable development and job creation. If the fiscal system is to be used to assist regional development, then regional rates on corporate income tax might be considered to help spread industrial activity and reduce present tendencies to geographic concentration. This has been a major cause of regional disparity and a threat to the quality of life in the overcrowded industrial areas of our country.

But much more significant in terms of increased revenue for the federal treasury and new direction to Canada's industrial strategy, if Canada may be said to have an industrial strategy at this time, are the items that would become taxable.

I see no reason for continuing the capital-cost allowance provisions. These must be changed so that allowable deductions are brought closer to depreciation provisions considered to be good accounting practice. That is simply to say that a company's income-tax return should show the same depreciation as does the annual report to shareholders.

In 1969, capital-cost allowance exceeded depreciation reported to shareholders by $677 million. If this had been subject to the approximately 50 per cent rate of tax applicable in 1969, the corporate-tax saving would have amounted to about $339 million. This is a substantial sum in one year—a sum which had to be made up by the individual taxpayer. Not all of this amount would be recoverable through amendments to the Income Tax Act. Removing this loophole would have resulted in a revenue increase of about $140 million in 1969, and more substantial increases later.

Special concessions to the mining and petroleum industry must end. These are the least justifiable concessions of all, in terms of job creation or long-range economic benefits to our country. They have served to divert capital from secondary industry, which does create considerable employment, and they have encouraged foreign-owned companies to gorge themselves on our precious, non-renewable natural resources. The amounts involved here are even larger than those in the preceding paragraph.

We propose to end the accelerated depreciation provisions that have been substituted for the three-year tax holiday. Depletion allowances of all types should no longer be permitted. Mining and petroleum companies should be made to pay for the right to exploit our minerals rather than deducting payments from their tax bill because the resource will run out. If our resources are depleted, it is we, the people, who suffer, not the companies. The companies pack up and move on. We are left with the ghost towns, the unemployed, the defaced landscape—the grim reality behind the word "depletion."

Thought should be given to a new category of deductible expenses for mining corporations. Certain sums should be set aside each year in anticipation of the closing of mines. These would provide for the cleaning-up of the mine site, early retirement benefits for workers who choose that option, and relocation expenses of those who do not. The extraction companies should be expected to provide for the wide range of possible disruptions that occur when a mine dies, and such provision would be a legitimate deduction because it would be part of the miners' security and that of their community. Mr. Turner's "ghost towns," after all, have not been created by the New Democratic Party. They have been created by the lack of government foresight that has given the extraction industries carte blanche to exhaust our resources without thought of the people's or community's future.

In 1969 depletion allowances reduced taxable income by $207 million. Exploration and development expenses charged against taxable income totalled $742 million. As a result ordinary Canadian taxpayers had to make up for $350 million in taxes because of these senseless provisions.

Investment by the corporation of community reserves such as I have described should be subject to guidelines established by the government to protect the interests of the mining communities and their citizens. For example, some portion of the reserve might be invested in the Canada Development Corporation.

In 1969, corporations reported $640 million in capital-gains income. None of it was included in taxable income then; half will be included in the tax year of 1972. Because it was not taxed in 1969, $250 million in federal revenue had to be drawn from these familiar victims of our tax system, people who received their income from labour instead of investments.

We propose the introduction of a full capital-gains tax for corporations. After reluctantly acknowledging that capital-gains income should be subject to tax, it is incredible that anyone with a sense of justice or a shred of common sense could argue that only half of such income be considered taxable. One of the flaws of preferential tax treatment for capital gains is that corporations and their shareholders manoeuvre to get their income in the form of capital gains. Apart from the revenue loss and the distorted economic decisions that result, attempts in the Income Tax Act to stop this procedure have added to the already complex and arbitrary provisions of the act that satisfy no one.

I have often pondered about the special treatment accorded dividends. Is there any defensible reason other than the power of those who live by them? The loophole of tax-free intercorporate dividends should be closed by some form of withholding tax. It is worth noting that, again, we are talking about very substantial sums. In 1969, for example, corporations reported $1296 million in non-taxable dividends.

Secondly, the three provisions for distributing tax-free dividends provided by the "reformed" Income Tax Act should be removed. For example, full taxation of capital gains would end the distribution of tax-free dividends from capital surplus.

115

I know of no reason in justice or logic why dividend income should not be treated like any other income for tax purposes. The dividend tax credit of 33⅓ per cent should no longer apply. Had this been the case in 1969, the latest year for which taxation statistics are available, the government would have had an additional $120 million in revenue, which the ordinary taxpayer also had to make up.

So far I have only talked about 1969. A lot of money has flowed through the loopholes since then; some loopholes have been changed, and new ones have been added.

The total value of loopholes in 1969 was approximately $850 million from the taxation of corporations. The capital-gains loophole is now only half as large as it was in 1969. On the basis of the "reformed" system, $125 million potential tax remains uncollected.

If the tax reform of 1971 accomplished anything, it was quickly undone in John Turner's first budget on May 8, 1972.

Depletion allowances were made easier to "earn" by adding new types of eligible expenditures. Our estimate is that the government gave up about $22 million to the mining industry. That changes the mineral industry total to $370 million.

Capital-cost allowances were increased to 50 per cent for machinery and equipment in the manufacturing and processing industries. The result: a $200-million revenue loss in 1972 and $400 million in 1973. The cost of excessive capital-cost allowances totals $340 million.

The entire package of loopholes enumerated above results in the following annual loss of government revenue:

Excessive capital-cost allowances		$340 million
Concessions to mining industries		$370 million
Half taxation of capital gains		$125 million
Dividend tax credit		$120 million
	Total	$955 million

Let us for a moment assume that the twenty-year construction of the corporate welfare state had not occurred. Let us also assume that we are a government attempting to decide between competing demands. On one side we have the proponents of the corporate welfare state, the "louder voices"

116

that haunt our present government. You are by now familiar with them.

On the other side are the programs that have not been carried out over the past twenty years on the grounds that we could not afford them. And we are aware of some of the challenges of the future: the need for better housing, the need to control the cost of living, the need to create meaningful employment opportunities, the needs of our senior citizens, the need to ensure Canada's economic independence, and with it control of our economic future.

Which of these would you choose, a vast and costly system of corporate welfare such as we have now, or a fair tax system to ease your burden and improve your future?

For this is the choice. Canada has enormous resources to meet the legitimate needs of its people. But these resources are pocketed by a privileged few, though they are generated by the labours of many.

The vast majority of us fulfill our obligations to society, and we benefit in return from the many services that are provided collectively by our society. But a very few benefit out of all proportion to their contribution. And by permitting their contribution to be withheld indefinitely, we deprive Canada of the means to bring about long-overdue changes in our social priorities.

We are all victims to some extent of the corporate myth. It is difficult for some to realize that institutions were created to serve the needs of people; that they have no life or soul of their own; that they have only the amount of power that people accord them; that they can exert only the amount of influence that people are willing to tolerate.

Every day of our lives we arrive at a crossroad. Every day we make decisions that will affect the course of our lives to a greater or lesser degree. To choose the right road, we must first know where we want to go. We must identify our destination. Otherwise, we stand paralyzed at the crossroad, without progress in any direction.

No decision of any moment is simple or without conflict. But no achievement of any merit was ever accomplished by shirking decision, by apathy, by timidity or by lack of commitment to desired goals. Canadians must confront themselves with the evidence. They must weigh it carefully, because justice is not blind. Justice comes only to those who work for it, demand it, shout for it and proclaim its worth above other considerations.

These are not distant ideals or empty dreams. In many countries of the world they would be. Canada has the resources and the people to make these goals a reality. But the people must make the choice. The future is in their hands.

Together, by the millions, they can make theirs the louder voices.

Reprinted with permission of the *Toronto Star*

Tit for tat